The Strange Rebirth
of Liberal England

The Strange Rebirth of Liberal England

David Walter

POLITICO'S

First published in Great Britain 2003 by

Politico's Publishing, an imprint of

Methuen Publishing Limited

215 Vauxhall Bridge Road

London SW1V 1EJ

10 9 8 7 6 5 4 3 2 1

A CIP catalogue record for this book is available from the British Library.

ISBN 1 84275 077 1

Printed and bound in Great Britain by Creative Print and Design, Ebbw Vale.

Contents

Acknowledgements

I am very grateful to the very many Liberal Democrats and others who have given up their precious time to share their memories with me for this book. They include: Paddy Ashdown, Eric Avebury, Alan Beith, Duncan Brack, Menzies Campbell, Pratap Chitnis, Tim Clement-Jones, George Crozier, Tom Dale, Dee Doocey, Graham Elson, Andrew Gifford, Richard Grayson, Tony Greaves, Nick Harvey, Richard Holme, Simon Hughes, Russell Johnston, Trevor Jones, Charles Kennedy, Archy Kirkwood, Alan Leaman, Robert Maclennan, Alec McGivan, Tom McNally, Paul Medlicott, Stuart Mole, Dick Newby, Mark Oaten, John Pardoe, Candy Piercy, Keith Raffan, Chris Rennard, Sue Robertson, Bill Rodgers, Jackie Rowley, Adrian Slade, David Steel, Andrew Stunell, Celia Thomas, Jeremy Thorpe, Graham Tope, Geoff Tordoff, Paul Tyler, Gerald Vernon-Jackson, William Wallace, Shirley Williams and Des Wilson.

Menzies Campbell, Duncan Brack, Richard Grayson, Mark Oaten, Chris Rennard and Paul Tyler read through part or all of the manuscript and helped me avoid a great many errors. Any that remain are, of course, my own responsibility.

Sadly, two great Liberal Democrats, Roy Jenkins and Richard Wainwright, died just after I embarked on this project, and before I was able to consult them. The book is the poorer for it, as the party is the poorer for their loss.

There are many others who should be part of this story and who are not included. With more time and more space they would have been. My apologies to them.

I am very grateful to Politico's for taking on this venture, and to Sean Magee and Iain Dale there for all their support.

My thanks finally to my wife Pamela and my children Natalie and Peter for their unstinting support and encouragement.

Introduction

Commentators have begun to talk about the possibility of a sea change in British politics. Seventy years after the publication of George Dangerfield's *The Strange Death of Liberal England*, there are strong signs of rebirth of Liberalism – not just in England, but in Scotland and Wales as well. The alternation of power between Labour and the Conservatives which has persisted for the past eighty years can no longer be taken for granted. The Liberal Democrats have been enjoying consistently strong ratings in the opinion polls and they are breathing down the necks of some of the most senior Tories in their constituencies. The local elections of 2003 pointed to a very even three-way split between the parties. We have certainly left the two-and-a-half-party system of the early post-war decades well behind. The situation is volatile, but the Liberal Democrats could well prove to be a more significant force in British politics in the twenty-first century than the Conservatives.

It is a worry which increasingly preoccupies the Conservative Party itself. Leading Tories like Francis Maude, Steve Norris, Kenneth Clarke and Michael Heseltine have all warned that the Liberal Democrats could overtake their party. Prominent members of the Conservative Shadow Cabinet like Theresa May and Michael Howard, whose seats are vulnerable to the Liberal Democrats on small swings, have been seen making desperate efforts to shore up their increasingly precarious-looking local power bases.

Yet we have been here before. The Liberal Party was briefly ahead of both Labour and the Conservatives in the polls in the aftermath of the Orpington by-election of 1962. In the early 1970s, the Liberals won five by-elections in rapid succession and seemed once again to be heading towards a breakthrough. Then there was the most dramatic advance of all. In the early 1980s, in the first flush of excitement surrounding the creation of the SDP, the Alliance of Liberals and Social Democrats was actually attracting more support than both the other parties put together. The Alliance led all opinion polls for a period of six months.

All these revivals were accompanied by suitably revivalist language. 'I intend to march my troops towards the sound of gunfire,' said Jo Grimond in 1963. 'We are going for a landslide,' predicted Jeremy Thorpe in 1974. 'Go back to your constituencies and prepare for government,' David Steel exhorted the party in 1981.

The SDP set out with the object of breaking the mould of British politics. Roy Jenkins, its first Leader, was fond of talking about 'the big breakthrough'. When the party was at its zenith, briefings and press conferences by Jenkins were big news. Any appearance by Jenkins had the quality of a well-rehearsed dramatic performance, an effect enhanced by his idiosyncratic pronunciation. At the end of one audience with the great man, a puzzled lady Canadian journalist who had been sitting at the back asked, 'Mr Jenkins, can you explain exactly what you mean when you talk about the big grapefruit?'

Somehow, though, the big grapefruit has as yet always stayed just a little too high up the tree for the Liberals, the Alliance or the Liberal Democrats to reach. But there has been a pattern to these revivals. Each time, the party has got a little nearer to the grapefruit, and each time, having just failed to grasp the prize, it has fallen slightly less far back down the tree. As the new century progresses, could the grapefruit really at last be attainable?

The current Liberal Democrat Leader Charles Kennedy is very conscious of the predictions unfulfilled in the past. One lesson which he has learnt from them is not to hype up the party's chances. But the prospects for the future do look more promising than they have been for a very long time.

This is a good moment, therefore to look back as well as forward, to examine the revivals of the past forty years and to consider where they succeeded and where they failed. There are lessons from the past which may apply in the current political climate and will effect the prospects for the future.

The difficulty which the Liberal Democrats and their predecessor parties have always had is that their fortunes have very seldom been in their own hands. Success or failure has usually depended on Tory swings and Labour roundabouts. Luck too is a commodity never to be underestimated in politics, particularly over the by-elections, which have always been particularly important to the third party. A vacancy in the right place at the right time has often meant a huge difference. Equally there have been setbacks because of forces over which no party has much control, like wars and the world economy.

The party's position has been that of a surfer, waiting patiently for the right wave to ride and then using all its skills to stay upright and to travel as far and as fast as possible. To that extent, it can control its own fortunes. In the past, it has missed some waves altogether and fallen off others. Sometimes it has looked in danger of being pulled underwater and never surfacing again. But it has also shown itself capable on occasions of achieving sufficient momentum and balance to get carried a very long way indeed.

My own involvement with Liberalism goes back to the 1960s. I remember being inspired by a lecture which Jo Grimond gave at my school, although sadly I have forgotten what he actually said. Like so many others of that period, I just remember the humour and the freshness of the approach, the charisma and the ability to engage with an audience of young people. Then, in the late 1960s, I was at Oxford

University through a period of great disillusionment with the Wilson Labour Government. I knew that I was not a Conservative. Hardly anybody was Labour. I found the rather more numerous Trotskyites ridiculous, especially those of their number who had been to Eton. That left the Liberals, who were strong in university politics at the time. I was particularly motivated by the strong and principled stance which the party was taking on issues like Vietnam, Rhodesia, apartheid and the rights of the Kenya Asians with British passports.

After university and a brief period of apostasy as a Labour supporter, I found myself in broadcasting, and learnt the discipline of political objectivity. In BBC local radio, I covered my first by-elections in Kingston upon Thames and Sutton and Cheam. I moved to national radio between the two 1974 general elections, and later in television tracked the course of the Lib–Lab pact as Professor Robert McKenzie's producer on *Nationwide*. Then in 1980, I joined ITN as a political correspondent, and was assigned to cover the momentous events surrounding the birth of the SDP and the Alliance. I heard Roy Jenkins make his key speech to the parliamentary press gallery. I was at the two Labour Party Conferences in Blackpool and Wembley which sealed the decision of the Gang of Three to leave Labour. I rode the famous 'train of shame', which carried the first rolling SDP Party Conference from Perth to Bradford to London. Then I began acquiring further by-election campaign medals. I was at Warrington, Croydon North West, Hillhead, Beaconsfield, Bermondsey and Darlington, then in the following Parliament at Stafford, Portsmouth South and Greenwich. I also covered the general elections of 1983 and 1987. I was at the Ettrick Bridge Summit in 1983, and like all the other journalists present missed the real story.

Later, my broadcasting portfolio began to widen, and I spent time making programmes on the European continent as much as in Britain. But I returned regularly to report on first the Alliance and then the

Liberal Democrats. In 1993, I narrated a fly-on-the-wall documentary about the Newbury by-election, where the party gave the BBC exclusive access behind the scenes. The film's big star was the Campaigns Director Chris Rennard, who was followed so continuously by our camera that he began to have nightmares about the crew filming him as he slept. He revealed afterwards that the real decisions had nonetheless been taken off camera in the local Indian restaurant, after the film unit had packed up for the day.

By 1998, I felt that broadcasting was becoming increasingly less enjoyable. Out of the blue, the Liberal Democrat Chief Whip Paul Tyler asked if I would consider becoming Director of Media Communications for the party. The idea grew on me and I accepted. I have worked for the party in various guises ever since, first under Paddy Ashdown and then under Charles Kennedy.

What follows therefore draws considerably on my own experience first from the outside and then from the inside. Although the events which I describe are seen through the eyes of a Liberal Democrat, I have tried to write history rather than propaganda.

So I neither start nor end with a great prediction. I do not forecast that the Liberal Democrats are at last poised to break the mould of politics. I do believe, however, that history demonstrates that the circumstances may be more favourable for them to do so now than ever before.

1   Going Down,
1910–45

A book about Liberal and Liberal Democrat revivals requires some account of the decline which made a revival necessary. It is certainly worth examining what there was left to revive, and indeed whether it was worth reviving. The history of the disintegration of the old Liberal Party may also offer some pointers to the dangers which face the modern Conservative Party.

Historians argue about what caused the eclipse of the Liberal Party. They divide into a Great War faction, which claims 1914–18 as the key period, and a class-war faction, which places the decisive developments in the pre-war era. The first major foray into the debate, George Dangerfield's *The Strange Death of Liberal England,* was published in 1935, a year in which it would have been reasonable to say that the chances of there ever being a Liberal Government again were extremely remote.

Dangerfield belongs firmly in the class-war camp. He dates the real crisis of Liberalism back to the four years between the death of Edward VII and the outbreak of the First World War, painting a picture of three forces advancing on the Liberal Government which it was powerless to control.

The first of these forces was the Conservative Party, with its allies in Ulster, who combined to pose a great threat to order as the Liberal

Party sought to introduce Home Rule for Ireland. The second force was the women's suffrage movement. The third and most significant was the working class which, as it became more unionised and class-conscious, saw the Liberals as referees rather than protagonists in the class struggle.

The rival Great War theory was notably championed by Trevor Wilson in his 1966 book *The Downfall of the Liberal Party*. Wilson argues that the party was run over by 'the rampant omnibus of war'. Liberal beliefs did not square easily with fighting wars, and the resulting strain caused the splits in the party which were to prove so damaging.

The two historical camps remain evenly matched. Dangerfield certainly still has staunch supporters. Detailed work on the electoral performance of the Liberal Party before the Great War has suggested that it continued to flourish only because a disproportionate number of working-class people did not have the vote. Where more of them were enfranchised, Labour performed much better, particularly in municipal elections. When eventually in 1918 the entire male population over twenty-one was given the vote, that sealed the Liberal Party's fate.

Certainly, once the glory days of the Edwardian era had passed, the Liberal Party entered a period of great political turbulence. Ireland was an increasingly large preoccupation. Under Andrew Bonar Law, the Conservative Party which was supposed to be the champion of law and order and of the British constitution, was fomenting civil war to prevent the Home Rule plans of the Liberal Government. Law's ally Sir Edward Carson had half a million followers ready to take up arms. On 28 November 1913, Law made a speech in Dublin which amounted to an incitement to the British forces to mutiny. Drawing a parallel with the war between James II and William of Orange, he said, 'In order to carry out his despotic intention, the King had the largest army which had ever been seen in England. What happened? There was no civil war. Why? Because his own army refused to fight for him.'

Dangerfield's charge against the Liberal Government is that in the face of the threats from Carson and his Tory allies, ministers equivocated and temporised, thereby losing the confidence of Irish Nationalists without reconciling the Ulster Protestants. The charge may have some validity against the Asquith Government, although there are few subsequent administrations which can be said to have covered themselves in much greater glory over the Irish question. But the charge does not hold against Liberalism itself. The concepts of decentralisation and Home Rule are central to Liberal philosophy. If Asquith had achieved Home Rule for Ireland during this period, it might well have prevented a great deal of bloodshed later.

At the same time, the Liberals faced other problems. Looking ninety years back and with the benefit of hindsight, it is hard to imagine why a Government espousing Liberal principles seemed reluctant to give women the vote. In the case of Ireland, the Government had the principles but not the determination to carry them out. Over female suffrage, the principles were not there in the first place. It is particularly hard to excuse the forced feeding which the suffragettes were made to undergo when they went on hunger strike in prison.

It can be said in the Government's defence that ministers eventually did come round to the idea of women's suffrage, albeit in the wish to keep the peace rather than out of fundamental commitment. It is also true that their opposition to giving women the vote was shared by a substantial minority of the emerging Labour Party. Fifteen Labour MPs were against it. The history of the suffragette movement does not wholly support the theory that the Liberals abandoned the torch of radicalism to the Labour Party.

In other ways, the Liberal Government was genuinely radical. It had introduced great social reforms, providing pensions, unemployment insurance and a degree of free health care. These advances on their own, however, could not guarantee the loyalty of the working classes. This was a period in which real wages were falling, despite the increased prosperity of the country. Labour increasingly seemed to be the only dependable champion to whom working men could turn.

Dangerfield writes of the poet Rupert Brooke, conjuring up a bygone age of 'honey still for tea' which represented Liberal England. It was a time when politics was a more gentlemanly pursuit. Leading figures on the Liberal and Conservative sides would argue with each other in the Commons, but remain on the closest social terms with each other outside it. By and large, they came from the same kind of privileged backgrounds. They had been to the same schools and universities.

By 1914, the relationship between the two sides had soured. Margot Asquith was outraged not to be invited to a ball given by Lord Curzon, at which the King and Queen were present. But the situation in Ireland meant that the Conservatives and Liberals effectively regarded each other as traitors. The stage was set for a much rougher kind of politics, which required rougher operators and was to endure for most of the twentieth century. It is hard to imagine the late Caroline Benn being upset at the lack of a ball invitation from Norman Tebbit.

However, it is not clear that the Liberal Government was notably more effete and dilettantish than its political opponents. Asquith may have opened himself up to the accusation which is sometimes levelled at his successor Charles Kennedy of being too laid back. He was not the only member of the Government to face such charges; the Chief Secretary for Ireland Augustine Birrell earned himself the nickname of 'The Playboy of the Western World'. But the Government also contained Churchill and Lloyd George, who could be accused of many things but hardly of being supine. And there were many senior Conservatives who were equally semi-detached from the task in hand. It was an era when life in general was a great deal more leisurely if you happened to have been born into the right class.

Nevertheless, Victorian and Edwardian Liberalism was ill equipped to deal with the new politics of class which were emerging. There were many lost opportunities. The Labour movement in its early days was not committed to maintaining a separate political party. Before the Labour Party was founded, trade union MPs sat as Liberals. If the Liberals had adopted more trade union candidates, they might have prevented the emergence of the Labour Party altogether, or at least narrowed its appeal. Instead, in the crucial period from 1888 to 1899, when the unions more than doubled their membership, the number of trade union Liberal MPs only increased from eight to eleven.

Even after the Labour Party had been formed, some trade unionists continued to sit as Liberals. The Miners' Union, for instance, only switched allegiance from Liberal to Labour in 1909. Labour was unable to attain a foothold in Parliament without electoral pacts. Ramsay Macdonald agreed a secret deal with the Liberals in 1903 which led to Labour winning thirty seats at the 1906 election. Labour were to remain dependent on Liberal goodwill until the First World War. At the 1910 election, no Labour candidate won in a three-cornered contest.

It was not until 1918 that the Labour Party officially adopted socialist objectives, with the commitment to 'secure for the producers by hand or by brain the full fruits of their industry and the most equitable distribution thereof'. Not long before that, Lenin had described the British trade unions as 'insular, aristocratic, selfish and hostile to socialism', and trade unionists continued heavily to outnumber socialists in the Labour Party for years to come.

The greatest gift which the Liberal Government gave Labour was the 1913 Trade Union Act. This allowed the unions to collect a political levy from their members. Overnight, the Labour Party's income became ten times larger. It is one of the ironies of history that the famous Millbank machine which won Labour the 1997 and 2001 general elections could not have existed without the generosity of a Liberal Government.

The Liberals could have tried to strangle the infant Labour Party at birth. The argument for tolerating it was that by making an accommodation with Labour, the Liberals could widen their appeal to the working-class electorate and thereby strengthen the anti-Conservative forces. Hence the pacts and the helpful legislation. Nobody foresaw that Labour would eclipse so rapidly a party which had won three general election victories in succession.

The Labour Party was certainly not the only factor in the decline of the Liberals. Several prominent Liberals left to join the Conservative Party, most notably Winston Churchill. Their main motive was fear of Bolshevism, against which the Tories appeared to be the only reliable bulwark.

To a very considerable extent, moreover, the Liberals destroyed themselves. The rift between Asquith and Lloyd George would not have assumed such devastating proportions if it had not taken place against the background of the First World War. It has even been suggested that it could have been prevented if it had not been for a bad oyster. The Liberal Chief Whip Percy Illingworth, said to have been the one person who could have reconciled the two great men, died after making a fatal gastronomic decision.

Once the rift began, it escalated inexorably. First, as the war effort appeared to flag, Lloyd George replaced Asquith as coalition Prime Minister. Then Asquith decided to sit as Leader of the Opposition. Next, the Asquithians championed the charges of the former Director of Military Operations Maj-Gen Sir Frederick Maurice, who claimed that the Government had misled the country about British military strength in France. The Asquithians caused great acrimony by dividing the House against the Government. Finally, the two Liberal groups fought the 1918 election on opposite sides, with Lloyd George in coalition with the Conservatives at the head of 150 coupon National Liberals and Asquith heading the independent Liberal Party. With his party down to thirty MPs, Asquith lost the East Fife seat which he had held for thirty-two years. It was not until 1987 that Menzies Campbell was to recapture it for Liberalism.

The inter-war history of the Liberal Party repeated a pattern of splits and reconciliations. There was a brief period of internal peace in 1923, when the Tory party was proposing tariffs and the Liberals united under their old banner of free trade. Yet by the early 1930s, there were no fewer than three separate Liberal forces in the Commons, the official party under Herbert Samuel, a group led by Sir John Simon which was heading rapidly towards integration with the Conservatives, and a small group of supporters of Lloyd George, mainly consisting of his relations.

The Liberals were not short of good policy ideas. John Maynard Keynes and Sir William Beveridge were both Liberals. Keynes pointed the way to economic recovery after the depression. Beveridge developed the blueprint for the post-war welfare state. The Liberal voice of internationalism continued to be heard over foreign affairs. The pre-war and wartime leader Archibald Sinclair, grandfather of the current MP for Caithness and Sutherland John Thurso, was one of the boldest and most outspoken opponents of appeasement.

Nevertheless the disputes between the leaders caused enormous electoral damage to the Liberal Party. It was providing a classic illustration of the law of politics, which states that the more a party shrinks the more divided it becomes. The experience of British politics has shown again and again that the electorate punishes divided parties. It was a lesson discovered in turn by all parties in the 1980s and 1990s, first by Labour, then by the Alliance and finally by the Conservatives.

The other enduring issue which first surfaced in the period before the First World War is the relationship between the Liberal and Labour Parties. For most of the twentieth century, with the exception perhaps of the 1940s and 1950s, the Liberals have seen themselves as outright opponents of the Conservatives but as competitors with the Labour Party for the centre-left vote. The tradition in Britain has tended to differ from the trend on the continent. The predominant strand of Liberal opinion in the UK has been of social liberalism, which shares many of the attitudes of social democracy. Social liberalism endorses the fundamental liberal principle of individual freedom, but holds that freedom can only be exercised if an enabling State guarantees high-quality public services. It has been the inspiration alike for Lloyd George's pensions, for Beveridge's National Health Service and for Ashdown's penny on income tax for education.

The fiercest disputes within Liberal ranks have revolved round the relationship with Labour. Some have worked for a realignment of the forces of the centre-left. Jo Grimond talked in these terms in the early 1960s. David Steel took the Liberal Party into the Lib–Lab pact and into the Alliance with the SDP. Paddy Ashdown was preparing for coalition with Tony Blair both before and after the 1997 general election. Others have been zealous defenders of a Liberal independence which they have seen as jeopardised by these initiatives and have resisted very forcefully.

In truth, however, the success or failure of any of these relationships has always lain far more in the hands of the Labour Party than of the Liberals. The one factor which could transform the situation would be the introduction of proportional representation, which has always been a strong motivation for Liberals and Liberal Democrats for entering into any relationship with Labour.

For years, the party's position towards the Labour Party was the only aspect of the Liberals or the Liberal Democrats which really interested the media. It is only very recently that journalists have started to pay serious attention to the policies of the Liberal Democrats in their own right.

Eighty-five years on from the 1918 election, the pieces of the political jigsaw are much rearranged, and for the most part in favour of Liberalism. The politics of class, which became so important then, are fading fast. Socialism is discredited. The serious internal divisions in today's politics afflict the Conservative and Labour Parties rather than the Liberal Democrats. Meanwhile, the ideas which inspired the great social reforms of those Liberal Governments continue to inform Liberal Democrat policy-making.

Liberals can look back to Gladstone's inspiration on Home Rule, to Lloyd George's creation of the old-age pension and to Beveridge's vision of the National Health Service. It is not a bad legacy to have.

2 Orpington Man, 1945–64

In the first ten years after the Second World War, it was touch and go whether the Liberal Party would survive at all. The party leader Sir Archibald Sinclair, who had served as Secretary of State for Air in the wartime coalition, lost his Caithness and Sutherland seat in the 1945 election, at which only twelve Liberal MPs were elected to Parliament. That figure was reduced further to nine in 1950. The general election of the following year, 1951, proved almost fatal. Only six Liberal MPs were returned, and of them only Jo Grimond had a Conservative opponent. If the others had faced three-cornered fights, the total would have been even lower. The party was down to 2.5% of the national vote. It fielded only 109 candidates with a mere forty-three so much as saving their deposits. The percentage vote in the seats contested scraped into double figures, but even so the party could easily have disappeared altogether.

Sir Winston Churchill, Prime Minister again in 1951, offered the Liberal Leader Clement Davies a seat in the Cabinet as Education Secretary, with two junior posts for other Liberals. Rejecting the advice of Asquith's daughter Lady Violet Bonham Carter, Davies decided not to enter the Government. If he had done so, that could have been the final straw for the Liberal Party which would have lost its remaining distinctiveness.

In the event, 1951 proved to be the nadir of the Liberals' fortunes, but recovery was slow. At the 1955 election, the same six MPs were returned, but with fractionally more of the popular vote and a few more good second places. The revival only began to gather pace when Jo Grimond was elected Leader in 1956 at the age of 43. A charismatic figure with huge charm, Grimond developed two themes which were to feature prominently in later revivals of the twentieth century.

The first was an appeal to voters who did not feel that they fitted into the old politics of class. As early as 1955, he talked about a new type of voter living 'in a land between the old working and the old middle classes'. The second, allied idea was for the realignment of the left. He believed that Liberals could make common cause with those Labour supporters who were neither Communist fellow travellers nor right-wing machine politicians tied to the trade union block vote. He also thought that there was scope for including liberal Conservatives in this realignment, but he was clearly repositioning the party on the centre-left. Hitherto, in the post-war era, it had been regarded as significantly closer to the Conservatives.

Grimond was good at stimulating ideas. He identified the party clearly with a number of causes, notably membership of the European Community, devolution for Scotland and Wales, colonial freedom and industrial democracy. The Liberals were once again assuming the role which they had played during the heyday of Beveridge and Keynes as pioneers of policies which were subsequently to be implemented by other parties. Electoral success for their own cause was to prove considerably more illusive.

The first year of Grimond's leadership showed the precarious nature of the Liberal recovery. He gained prominence for his powerful critique of Eden's Suez policy. Grimond was against the Suez expedition almost from the outset, while the Labour Leader Hugh Gaitskell sat on the fence. In Parliament, most of the rest of the small parliamentary Liberal Party followed their Leader's line. But one of them, Sir Rhys Hopkin Morris, was resolutely pro-Eden. When Sir Rhys died suddenly in

November 1956, his constituency Liberal Association in Carmarthen selected another supporter of the Suez adventure as the prospective candidate. Grimond found himself reluctantly campaigning for a standard-bearer with whom he disagreed profoundly on the main issue of the day. The seat was duly lost to Labour, whose candidate was none other than Lloyd George's daughter Megan. This was not the last time that a bad choice of by-election candidate was to halt the party's advance.

Carmarthen, however, was amongst the one-step-backs of the time which went alongside several two-steps-forwards. Grimond was the first politician truly to master television, and his effectiveness on the medium stood the Liberals in very good stead. He made Liberal policy positions sharper and more distinctive on questions like reform of the House of Lords and devolution of power. And he raised the sights of the party. At the Southport Liberal Assembly in 1958, he said, 'I am not prepared to lead a party of eunuchs. They must be a serious campaigning party, interested in power and influence, not a brains' trust.'

One consequence was that fresh talent was attracted to the Liberals. The broadcasters Ludovic Kennedy and Robin Day were both selected as candidates. Menzies Campbell, one of those first attracted to the party during the Grimond era, remembers the ITN newscaster Kennedy and his film star wife Moira Shearer adding great excitement and glamour to the Liberal cause. At the 1958 by-election in Rochdale, Ludovic Kennedy pushed the Conservatives into third place and came within 5,000 of Labour. It prompted Lord Hailsham to attack the Liberals as 'usurpers; a party without a policy, an aim, an outlook or a philosophy', Hailsham was sufficiently shaken by this result to offer his resignation to Harold Macmillan. In refusing to accept it, Macmillan suggested to his Party Chairman that it might be wiser to try and woo Liberals than to attack them.

Then, shortly afterwards, the Liberals won Torrington, the first by-election gain for the party since March 1929, when James Blindell won Holland-with-Boston. The victorious candidate was Mark Bonham Carter, Asquith's grandson and Grimond's brother-in-law. Torrington was a great achievement. It was not, however, a very lasting one. The seat was lost again at the 1959 general election, where the success of the by-election may nonetheless have clinched a narrow victory for Jeremy Thorpe in next-door North Devon.

Grimond's own political stance was clear. He talked about carving out a niche to the left of centre 'in the sense that we stand for personal freedom against authority and in the sense that we believe there is still too much poverty, too many slums and too much cruelty and in the sense that we want and mean to have a wide dispersal of property and power'.

There was much less coherence about the Liberal Party as a whole. Robin Day, who fought Hereford in 1959, but whose views were subsequently to move to the right, complained that 'as an organisation, the Liberal Party was a shambles ... it was likely to be hopelessly divided between the old traditionalists and the young radicals ... To many of its supporters it was a party of the reasonable centre. To many of its activists it was a party of the militant left. A political party could be either of these, but not both.'

Incoherence in policy was accompanied by weakness in organisation. In 1959, Jo Grimond himself and the other MPs decided that they were individually too vulnerable to defeat to spend much time campaigning outside their own constituencies. It was difficult to mount much of a national campaign on that basis.

Nevertheless, the 1959 general election showed a marked improvement on 1955. Overall, the Liberals won 5.9% of the vote. They fought 216 constituencies with only fifty-six lost deposits. In the seats contested in both 1955 and 1959, their vote went up from 15.1% to 16.9%. In the aftermath of the election, Grimond made organisational changes at party headquarters to streamline the party machine. The conditions were ripe for a much more significant breakthrough in the new Parliament.

By 1962, the other two parties were in trouble. Labour had been through bruising encounters over unilateral disarmament and national-isation, with the leader Hugh Gaitskell looking increasingly beleaguered by the party's left. Equally the shine was coming off the Macmillan Government. Particularly unpopular was the pay pause of the Chancellor, Selwyn Lloyd, which meant that nurses were to be denied the modest pay increase that they had been expecting.

In comparison with both the Conservatives and Labour, Jo Grimond's Liberals looked fresh and untarnished. Grimond was a great iconoclast who was fond of debunking the establishment. He had a strong appeal to the new Sixties generation, who were to embrace the satire boom. As early as the Eastbourne Liberal Assembly of 1960, the party had seen a large rise in turnout, with 800 of the 1,100 delegates aged under forty. This marked a huge contrast with the years before Grimond's leadership, when the average age of Liberal members had been rising to the point at which it seemed that in due course the party would literally die out.

The Liberals were recruiting strongly in the universities. William Wallace, now Lord Wallace of Saltaire, was among many who joined at the time. When he was President of the Cambridge University Liberal Club in 1961, it had 1,200 members, more than either its Conservative or its Labour counterpart. Paul Tyler, another active Liberal student, remembers how much more attractive to students Grimond seemed than Hugh Gaitskell did.

Furthermore, the party was beginning to become more professional. After the 1959 general election, it had established a local government department, under Pratap Chitnis. Until now, there had been no attempt to co-ordinate the efforts of the Liberal councillors scattered around the country. Chitnis understood the importance of developing the party's strength from the grass roots, and of building on council election successes to win parliamentary seats. During his time, Liberals began to make a particularly significant impact locally in Liverpool, Southend, North-East Lancashire and Birmingham, where a pioneering grass roots campaigner called Wallace Lawler was to win a by-election in 1969.

It was grass roots strategy which was to prove decisive at Orpington, although the party was also helped by a series of errors made by the Conservatives. The vacancy arose when the sitting MP Donald Sumner resigned to become a county court judge. Subsequent electoral history has shown that, while voters are sympathetic to a party defending a seat because of an MP's death, they are apt to punish it when the member has gone off voluntarily to a more comfortable or better rewarded job. The Conservatives clearly had not imagined that Orpington was anything other than a very safe seat. The general election majority had been 14,760.

Secondly, it appeared that the Conservatives were keen to ease Mr Sumner out of the seat so that they could get a Central Office high flyer called Peter Goldman into Parliament. Such carpet-bagging was greatly resented in Orpington. Previous Conservative MPs had always had a strong affinity with the constituency and had been seen as spokesmen for the local community. Goldman made matters worse by campaigning by caravan. He would sit in the caravan while his supporters knocked on doors and asked electors if they wanted to meet him. The voters formed the impression that he could not be bothered to walk up their front paths. He was behaving as if he was their anointed MP and that it would be a great privilege for them to meet him.

Thirdly, and most fatally, the Conservatives delayed moving the writ for the by-election. They left the seat vacant for five and a half months, and then only went ahead after Jeremy Thorpe had presented a petition in Parliament on behalf of 3,502 Orpington voters. The delay gave the

Liberals invaluable time to consolidate their position in the constituency.

Alongside these negative factors for the Conservatives, there were a number of positive advantages for the Liberals. The main one was that they had put in seven very hard years' work building up a local government base. Following a lost deposit in the 1955 election, they formed ward organisations and started to fight council elections. They were able to capitalise on strong local issues like the opposition to giving Orpington the status of a separate borough, the lack of shops and amenities and feelings about high council house rents. Meanwhile, Liberal membership was growing and fund-raising events began to put the local party on a sounder financial footing. Social activity undoubtedly helped to sustain the membership. In his memoir of the campaign *The Orpington Story*, one of the local stalwarts Donald Newby writes, 'Our parties after the election counts started in 1957 and got gayer every year.'

At the 1959 council elections, the Liberals finally won two seats and went on to come within 500 votes of second place at the general election. By 1961, the council group had swollen to twelve, and the Conservatives were sounding rattled. Sumner said at the Conservative Annual General Meeting, 'The Liberal Party in Orpington will be defeated by their own false promises and false criticisms of Orpington Council.' Tory literature accused the Liberals of mendacity. The Liberals relished the attacks; they saw them as useful extra publicity.

By the time it was announced that Donald Sumner was to become a judge, the Orpington Liberals were well established. They faced one very substantial problem. It emerged that the candidate who had fought the 1959 election, Jack Galloway, had remarried before the decree absolute had come through from his first marriage. It was an innocent mistake, but there was a danger that Galloway's first wife might put in unhelpful appearances at Liberal by-election meetings. The party felt that charges of bigamy were better kept out of the campaign. Pratap Chitnis went around the constituency making sure that the ward parties were lined up to deselect Galloway. At one point, when the outcome looked particularly doubtful, Chitnis happened to be visiting the Leeds constituency of the Chief Whip Donald Wade, in whom he confided. Wade suggested that perhaps it might be best not to fight the by-election at all.

Ultimately, with the wretched Galloway sitting outside the meeting in his car, the Orpington Liberals voted to find another candidate. The choice fell on the thirty-three-year-old Eric Lubbock. He had joined the party only two years before but had recently been elected to the council. In the light of the problems with Galloway, it would have been a catastrophe for the Liberals if the by-election had not been so delayed. Chitnis marvelled at the incompetence of the supposedly all-powerful Conservative Central Office machine.

Lubbock was able to conduct a very thorough canvass of the constituency before the campaign proper began. He was personable, with a young family, and proved very adept at harnessing local issues to the Liberal cause. The techniques of community politics are generally considered to have been invented a decade or so later, but this is effectively what the Orpington Liberals were doing from the late 1950s onwards. Eric Lubbock (now Lord Avebury) says:

> I've always said, and I think this is strongly borne out by history since then, that unless you start at that level and you can show people what they can achieve in their own day-to-day affairs – the ones that matter most to people – that you're not going to get their support at the parliamentary level. So you build that up. You've got councillors showing what they can do on the local authority and continuing to come round and liaise with local people, feeding back what they've managed to achieve, and that's the basis on which you're going to succeed at the parliamentary level.

> *We didn't talk about community politics. But that is what it was. At the 1966 count, my opponent Norris McWhirter said that he now understood that people were more interested in their back fences than in national politics. There was a sense in which that was true in that people did want a local MP who looked after their grievances about the roads and the commuter trains and the threats to the local hospital – everything that people related to in their day-to-day lives. Even though they might have had national implications.*

Francis Boyd, Political Editor of the *Guardian*, acknowledged the importance of this approach in his report of the Orpington victory. The result, he said, 'while it is a great personal tribute to the Liberal member, Mr Lubbock, is even more a reward to the rank and file of the party, not only in Orpington but throughout the country. The Liberals of Orpington have in the last year or two entered wholeheartedly into the campaign of the rank and file in other parts of the country to build up a party organisation from ward level and through the local government elections.'

Orpington was not the only place where the Liberals were working in this way. Chitnis was stimulating local campaigns all over the country. Often a hot issue would galvanise a local party into action. In Finchley, a council-owned golf course had a policy to exclude Jews as members. The MP, one Mrs Margaret Thatcher, was keeping her head down over the issue. The Liberals took up the cudgels and got the policy reversed. At the 1962 elections for the borough of Finchley, Liberal candidates swept the board. The young activist who led the campaign, John Pardoe, became the prospective parliamentary candidate.

Orpington, however, remained the paradigm for this approach. There was one memorable incident during the course of the by-election. Early in the morning of 25 February 1962, the Liberal Central committee rooms at the village hall caught alight. It took the fire brigade eighty minutes with five fire engines to get the flames under control. Eric Avebury recalls that 'as we surveyed the smoking ruins, somebody said to me, "I never thought that the Tories would go that far." And it was seriously suspected that this was an act of arson, although there was no proof of it. A lot of people suspected that it was actually my agent's careless habits with cigarette ends that caused the fire. He used to chuck them into the wastepaper basket, which is not very wise.'

In fact, the fire attracted very sympathetic national publicity, and proved a net benefit to the campaign. Furthermore, there were no canvassing records at the village hall. Miraculously, none of the Liberal posters were damaged either – the only posters burnt were Tory ones which the Young Liberals had removed the previous night. Jeremy Thorpe spirited the remains away in the boot of his car, and put them on a bonfire a safe distance outside the constituency.

Jo Grimond played an important role in the campaign himself. On 5 March, he attracted an audience of 470 to the largest political meeting ever held in Orpington. The next day the senior Conservative Iain Macleod drew only 200. On polling day, Jo Grimond and Eric Lubbock were lent a white Chevrolet to tour the constituency. 'We stood up in an open boot,' recalls Eric Avebury. 'Jo and I were hanging onto the inside of the boot lid and every time the car accelerated or slowed down, we had to do a rapid rebalancing act in this boot. And it was freezing cold. It was snowing on polling day and when we got back to the committee room we were absolutely frozen stiff.'

The *Daily Mail* was less impressed by the car than by Lubbock's footwear. It reported that in the boot of the car he was wearing his sixth pair of shoes: 'He wore out the other five tramping 350 miles to sell his "local boy" appeal.'

Orpington saw a thoroughly professional Liberal campaign, masterminded by the cigarette-smoking agent Pratap Chitnis. It foreshadowed the later by-election coups of the 1970s, 1980s and 1990s. Chitnis brought in two thousand Liberal volunteers during the course of the campaign. Young volunteers, sporting the local Liberal colour of Day-Glo green, were encouraged to get up on soapboxes all round the constituency and preach the message. On the final Saturday, Chitnis had far more volunteers than he could use. Rather than having to turn them away, he devised a strategy of telling the helpers who arrived in the north that they were needed in the south and vice versa, so that there was an impression of enormous Liberal activity all over the constituency and the volunteers could feel that they had done their bit.

On the eve of poll, the *Daily Mail* published an opinion poll showing that the Liberals were set to win. The *Mail* reported, 'It is not too late for the Conservatives to pull back success. Their party machinery is extremely efficient and may bring out more supporters to the polls. The very publication of this poll and the suggestion of a Liberal win could stir the Tories into a frenzy of work.' The poll also showed that, when people were asked whom they expected to win rather than who they wanted to win, 72.8% said the Conservatives.

Nonetheless, Chitnis was determined to use the poll to maximum Liberal advantage. He rounded up enough volunteers to deliver 5,000 copies of the paper in Labour areas to help squeeze the Labour vote. Then on polling day itself, he marshalled an enormous force of Liberal helpers. There were a thousand tellers at polling stations, quite apart from the hundreds of volunteers knocking at voters' doors.

The result was a sensation. Lubbock had polled 22,846 votes to Goldman's 14,991, a Liberal majority of 7,855 and a 32% increase in the Liberal vote. It sent shockwaves through the Conservative Party. Torrington had been won in the West Country, where the tradition of voting Liberal remained strong even in the party's bleakest days. Orpington was miles away from the Celtic fringe, in a London suburb which had seemed impregnably Tory. Macmillan complained that all the Government's efforts had only made Britain safe for Liberalism.

The political impact of Orpington was considerable. In his victory speech, Eric Lubbock said, 'This is not just a by-election victory. It is the start of a Liberal revival, the big breakthrough which could bring in the Liberal Party first as the main opposition, and then as the Government.' Press comment was more restrained, but nevertheless acknowledged the importance of the result. *The Times* called it 'the most significant blow that the Conservatives have suffered since they returned to office in 1951'.

Listing the second places which the party had achieved in the run-up to Orpington, *The Times* commented, 'These constituencies are so very mixed in type that Mr Grimond and his lieutenants can fairly claim that there is nothing freakish in their party's resurgence. There is a tide flowing their way just now. It may not be broad enough or strong enough to sweep Liberalism very far, but it is certainly proving powerful enough to be more of a nuisance to the two main parties than at any time since the end of the war.'

The jury remained out for the *Guardian* as well. Its leader noted, 'The country is saying, in effect, that it does not like the Government it has got, but is still a long way from deciding what alternative to choose.'

The Liberals had had a great deal of luck over Orpington, but they exploited that luck very skilfully and it was combined with a huge amount of hard work. Nevertheless, they proved unable to sustain their momentum up to the general election of 1964. Partly, they suffered from bad timing. The day before Orpington, they had just missed taking the seat of Blackpool North by under a thousand votes. If Blackpool had polled just after Lubbock's triumph instead of just before, it would almost certainly have been a second Liberal gain.

For a while, nonetheless, the Liberal bandwagon kept rolling. A national poll in the *Daily Mail*, a fortnight after Orpington, put the

Liberals ahead of both the Conservatives and Labour. There were outstandingly good council election results in May 1962. Then the momentum slowed when a lacklustre candidate missed West Derbyshire by 1,500 votes in June. Greater effort and a better standard-bearer might just have secured an all-important second victory, but the East Midlands was a weak area for the Liberals. The party was not yet a truly national party again, more a coalition of isolated regional power bases.

Nonetheless, the party scored another good second place in Leicester North-East, after which Macmillan decided on the famous 'night of the long knives', in which he sacked half his Cabinet. 'Greater love hath no man', said Jeremy Thorpe, 'than he lays down his friends for his life.'

There was much talk at the time of the phenomenon of Orpington Man, the new kind of voter who was willing to respond to Grimond's appeal for an end to the politics of class. In an interview after the result, in language which reflected the era, Jo Grimond said, 'There are some large factories in Orpington, doing electrical stuff. I think we got through to this difficult sort of chap, the new factory worker, not the miner, the New Man. He voted Liberal. And the young sort of chap. He voted Liberal. I admit though – and I'll be perfectly candid – that we got a considerable protest vote.' Eric Avebury elucidates:

> *Orpington might have been the beginning of the rejection of the social hierarchy which had been really part of our national politics right up to that moment. The Conservative Party was still dominated at that time by the scions of the landed aristocracy, the so-called knights of the shires and people who'd been to Eton or Oxford. People were fed up with the old idea of the domination of the Conservative Party because of their position in the hierarchy. It was the beginning of a revolution which is still going on creating an equal society. Then it was not so much a question of equality between different groups, but of equality between classes.*

But the same idea which Jo was then developing has been extended by our party to embrace all sections of the community. We think automatically of equality between genders, of equality between people of different religions and different races – people of different sexual orientation and disability and everything. So the class thing was the beginning of that trend I think.

Nonetheless, Lord Avebury rejects the idea that there was such a thing as Orpington Man:

I used to resent this in a way because it implied there was a cut-out figure who could be used to represent my constituents. And what happened was that the journalist used to arrive at the station and go along the station road and go into the Maxwell, which was the nearest pub to the station and then chat to a few people there and come back and think they knew what Orpington was and come back and describe the homogeneous figure who they believed had caused this upset.

Mr Macleod was nearer to it when he said the faceless people of Orpington had caused this result. Because there were actually a tremendous variety of people. There was St Mary Cray, which is entirely working class. There was Biggin Hill, which is a mixed community, and then there's the centre of Orpington, which conformed slightly more to their stereotype of a commuter with a bowler hat and umbrella working in the City, but even there – within the middle of Orpington, where all these commuters and bowler hats came from – were a lot of radicals, academics and people who had no connection with the world of commerce at all.

So this was a false impression which was created in the minds of the public, that you could somehow label the whole of the constituency with one single identity. And I don't think you can do that with any constituency. Orpington in particular was of enormous variety. It was the biggest constituency in Greater London by the way in terms of geographical area and probably one of the most varied.

By the end of 1962, Liberal Party support had fallen again to the low teens in the polls. The Orpington bubble had burst. Both the other two parties had begun to recover. The Conservatives developed some effective attacking literature against the Liberals. Iain Macleod published figures which suggested that there was a £4,000 million gap between the Liberals' plans for public expenditure and the amount which they proposed to raise in taxes. There was some substance to the charge. The party's policies were not subjected to the rigorous costings which they face today.

Jo Grimond continued to inspire his struggling troops, most notably with his famous speech to the Liberal Assembly in Brighton in 1963. 'In bygone days,' he told them, 'the commanders were taught that when in doubt they should march their troops towards the sound of gunfire. I intend to march my troops towards the sound of gunfire.' The party's rhetorical power was, sadly, not matched by organisational strength. The Liberals were much more efficient than they used to be, but they had nothing like the manpower or financial resources which their opponents could muster.

The party seemed very amateur at the time compared with its rivals. It was still small, too. William Wallace points out how little depth there was. You could meet all the senior people very quickly. Furthermore, many activists were still orientated towards endless policy discussion rather than towards the need to mobilise support and votes. Leafleting and canvassing were low on the list of priorities.

Another problem was the media. In 1960, both the *News Chronicle* and the *Star* ceased publication. Ever since then, there has been no national newspaper which has been an outright supporter of the Liberal Party or the

Liberal Democrats. Jo Grimond and his successors as party leaders have all been strong TV and radio performers. The print media, however, tend to set the political agenda far more than the broadcasters, and the lack of firm and dependable allies in what used to be Fleet Street has been a major weakness.

In the run-up to the 1964 election, none of the Liberal MPs felt secure enough to abandon their local power bases for long to go and campaign up and down the country, the victor of Orpington included:

> *People advised me very sensibly not to do too much of that but to make as much of a mark as I could locally and to concentrate on my own constituency. And I think the other MPs were in a similar position. Whereas nowadays people are free to campaign – even the ones with relatively small majorities don't feel it's incumbent on them to spend every single weekend going round the flower shows and the local events as we did in those days. I spent every Saturday and Sunday doing local things in the constituency and not campaigning up and down the country. So that may be another reason why we didn't succeed in exploiting what appeared to be a breakthrough.*

At the 1964 general election, few candidates campaigned on local issues in the way Eric Lubbock had done in Orpington. It was several years before the party learned how effective that approach could be for an insurgent third force in politics. Meanwhile, both the other two parties had changed Leaders. Jo Grimond had been very effective against Harold Macmillan; he found Sir Alec Douglas-Home a harder target. On the Labour side, Harold Wilson had become Leader on the death of Hugh Gaitskell. In the light of his subsequent career, it is sometimes forgotten how charismatic and popular Wilson was considered in his early years as Leader. Grimond's Liberals were inevitably thrust back into the shade as Wilson described how the white heat of technology would transform Britain.

Although Liberal support fell after Orpington, it did not fall back to the level of 1959. In the 1964 election, the number of Liberal MPs went up, albeit to the modest total of nine. Eric Lubbock was one of those who held his seat, despite being unable to call on all the national resources which he had at his disposal during the by-election. The attention which the by-election had brought the party, coupled with Jeremy Thorpe's skills as a fund-raiser, had helped to swell the party's coffers considerably. As a result, the party was able to fight the general election on a much more professional basis.

In many ways, Orpington was a model campaign which it took a long time for other constituencies to emulate. Nevertheless, the steady build-up from the local government base did create a blueprint which successful Liberal constituency parties eventually followed again and again.

The aftermath suggested that as yet the party was too small and too diffuse to make the most of the success. In Orpington, it could refute the notion that voting Liberal was a wasted vote, but this was much harder to challenge in many other constituencies. There was something, too, in the frequent charge from political opponents that the Liberals were a one-man band. The party's fortunes did depend to an enormous extent on the charisma of Jo Grimond.

The electorate, meanwhile, appeared to be voting Liberal in protest against the other parties, rather than as a positive statement in favour of Liberalism. Liberal successes caused the other parties to make changes, but when Conservatives and Labour adapted to the electors' concerns, their support started to return.

Nevertheless, Orpington remains a potent symbol for Liberals and Liberal Democrats of what they can achieve. The fortieth anniversary of the by-election was celebrated in style at the National Liberal Club, even though the party has not held the seat since 1970. In 2001, it was the narrowest of all the misses, and its recapture at the next general election is eagerly anticipated.

3   Six Million Votes, 1964–74

The 1960s were a much stronger decade for the Liberal Party than the 1950s. After Orpington, however, the era never presented another opportunity for a breakthrough on the same scale. It was more a question of modest and patchy progress. Three of the four gains of the 1964 election were in the Scottish Highlands, in Inverness, in Ross and Cromarty and in Caithness and Sutherland. The other was in Bodmin in Cornwall. Overall, the party had a net gain of three seats from the previous general election and won over three million votes.

This represented a significant advance. Grimond was a strong believer in devolution, and he highlighted the issue in the campaign. He told Sutherland Liberals, 'We are in an area not only far from London generally but also far from the thinking of people in London. If this was colonial territory, I sometimes think we would be more generously treated.' Even with the new gains, however, the party remained firmly anchored in the Celtic fringe. The Liberals might have held sway over 11,000 square miles of Highland territory from Muckle Flugga to Ballachulish, but they had made few inroads into areas where the sheep did not outnumber the people.

Between 1964 and 1966, it did seem possible that the party would break through in a different way. Labour had the narrowest of overall majorities. The nine Liberals were close to holding the balance of power. Jo Grimond began exploring the possibilities of a deal with Labour, earning the criticism of the more purist Liberals and dividing the parliamentary party for his pains. The parliamentary arithmetic never quite brought the issue to a head, but the question of co-operation with Labour was firmly on the Liberal agenda, and was to resurface in the party at regular intervals, generating great passion on both sides of the argument.

These battle-lines were to be drawn at least three more times after the 1964 Parliament: in 1977 over the Lib–Lab pact, in 1981 when the SDP was founded, and either side of the 1997 election when Paddy Ashdown was in talks with Tony Blair. Essentially the argument has remained the same. One side stresses the independence of the Liberal Party and the need to protect Liberalism from being diluted or swallowed up by illiberal politicians and their doctrines. The other side emphasises the opportunities to become more relevant in British politics and to advance liberal ideas by working with others. In particular, this argument stresses the potential for achieving a reform of the electoral system.

Ever since 1964, a very large proportion of the media coverage of the Liberals, the Alliance and the Liberal Democrats has concentrated on relations with other parties, mostly with the Labour Party. It is only now that we have reached the twenty-first century that this media preoccupation has faded.

Back in 1965, Jo Grimond's rather Delphic utterances about possible deals with Harold Wilson were given short shrift by the activists. The redoubtable Nancy Seear warned him at the autumn Liberal assembly not to go 'a-whoring after foreign women', and the initiative failed to go any further.

There was no by-election during that Parliament which quite rivalled the sensation of Orpington, but David Steel's 1965 victory in Roxburgh, Selkirk and Peebles was a very welcome boost to Liberal morale, bringing the party's tally of seats into double figures after a gap of fifteen years. The constituency included some traditional Liberal heartland; on former boundaries, it had been held by a Liberal as recently as the 1950–1 Parliament. Nonetheless, the result was a considerable success for the Liberal Party. It was also considered a fatal blow to the Tory Leader Sir Alec Douglas-Home, whose family seat was nearby; he resigned not long afterwards.

The 1966 general election saw a phenomenon which was to be repeated in the 1980s and 1990s. While the Liberal share of the national vote went down, partially though not entirely because the party fielded fewer candidates, the number of seats went up to twelve. The party established a precarious further toe-hold in urban Britain, with the victories of Dr Michael Winstanley in Cheadle and of Richard Wainwright in Colne Valley, as well as strengthening its position in the West Country with John Pardoe gaining North Cornwall.

The 1966–70 Parliament was potentially less promising for the Liberal Party. Labour had a majority of a hundred seats. There was no question of the twelve Liberals holding the balance of power even when Labour MPs revolted. Furthermore, Jo Grimond was wearying of the leadership. He had been in post for more than a decade with even less back-up than his successors were to enjoy. He was worried about his increasing deafness. Worst of all, in the middle of the 1966 election campaign, he had heard the dreadful news that his eldest son Andrew had committed suicide.

Liberal activists were desperately disappointed at Grimond's decision to resign. John Pardoe was one of many who tried in vain to persuade him to stay on, but Grimond's mind was firmly made up. The front-runner for the succession was Jeremy Thorpe. The practice was for the Leader to be elected by the parliamentary party. In 1956, there had not been a contest. In 1967, there were no fewer than three candidates amongst the twelve MPs: Thorpe, Eric Lubbock and Emlyn Hooson. In the first round, the votes split six for Thorpe and three for each of the others. The alternative vote system was no help. All Lubbock's second preferences were for Hooson and all Hooson's for Lubbock. The three candidates withdrew together to the whips' inner sanctum and Hooson and Lubbock then conceded to Thorpe. Whereas subsequent leadership elections have garnered the party publicity, which has been on balance favourable and helpful, this election made the Liberals look slightly ridiculous.

The twelve MPs nevertheless made some principled stands during the Parliament, especially in opposition to the Commonwealth Immigrants Act. This was directed at limiting the numbers of Kenyan Asians coming into Britain, despite the fact that they were full British-passport-holders who had good reason to flee Kenya. David Steel calls the Act in his book *Against Goliath* 'a most discreditable episode in our parliamentary history, a major concession to racism and a blot on the reputation of the Labour Party'.

The stance which the party took on the Kenya-Asian issue, along with its principled positions on Rhodesia, apartheid and race relations in Britain, underlined the need for a strong, distinctive liberal voice in British politics. There was little sign, however, that this would be anything other than a small minority voice of conscience. The Liberal Party was victim to a trend which it had felt before in 1950 and 1951 and was to feel again in 1979. When Labour's fortunes declined, the Liberals' prospects tended to diminish as well. The 2001 election was the first since the Second World War in which a decline in Labour support, albeit a small one, was accompanied by a rise in Liberal or Liberal Democrat vote share.

Jeremy Thorpe took time to establish himself as Leader. One veteran activist, Adrian Slade, believes that Thorpe was a good Leader against the Conservatives but hopeless against Labour. He had too good a relationship with Harold Wilson to be able to criticise the Prime Minister effectively. Thorpe also had a reputation as a lightweight to live down. Later, in the 1970s, when James Callaghan was Foreign Secretary, Thorpe went to brief him on a meeting which he had had with the rebel Rhodesian Premier Ian Smith. Callaghan was somewhat surprised to hear a verbatim account of the meeting in which Smith's side of the conversation was delivered entirely in Smith's voice. Thorpe was a superb mimic, but Callaghan wondered afterwards whether this was serious politics or a cabaret act.

Thorpe had his strengths nonetheless. He was brilliant as a public speaker, particularly in dealing with hecklers. He had a supreme confidence on the platform, which conveyed itself to almost any audience. The future MP Sir Archy Kirkwood, who was on the party staff in the early 1970s, remembers going with Thorpe to a Scottish Party Conference in St Andrews. The Leader arrived with not much time to spare, and announced that there was one thing which he really needed to do and that was to change his socks. Once the fresh socks were in place, his aide Richard Moore handed him a text for his speech. Then, without reading it through, he delivered it brilliantly to the audience, lifting the words from the page in a way that few could match.

On another occasion, Thorpe announced that he would do a party political broadcast about housing policy, an issue on which Thorpe's knowledge, according to Archy Kirkwood, would easily fit on a postage stamp and still leave a wide border. Kirkwood was asked to brief the leader, which he did for a few minutes while Thorpe, clad in a silk dressing gown, was brushing his teeth. Then they recorded the broadcast, which consisted of a number of leading experts on housing firing unscripted questions at the Liberal Leader. Thorpe was brilliant again. He was, as Kirkwood says, a magician; you could not tell how he did it. Shirley Williams believes that Thorpe's talents gave him the capacity to project the party as something far greater than it actually was. His sheer brilliance papered over the fact that its MPs were a collection of passionate individualists who gave the party little coherence as a whole.

However, Jeremy Thorpe had his critics. There was no clear idea about what he believed on a very wide range of subjects. And there was considerable doubt over the direction in which he was leading the party. In 1968, some leading activists were sufficiently impatient with Thorpe's leadership that they tried to stage a coup to bring back Jo Grimond. With an uncharacteristic touch of ruthlessness, it was timed to coincide with Thorpe's honeymoon. It was also a dismal failure. One of the many factors which undermined the plotters was that one of their number was a double agent, who was totally loyal to Thorpe and who regularly relayed details of the plotters' activities back to the Leader. When Thorpe returned, Lady Violet Bonham Carter, who was fiercely loyal to him, delivered a stinging rebuke to the plotters at a particularly well-attended meeting of the National Executive.

Two other developments of the late 1960s had a great bearing on subsequent history. One was the rise of the Young Liberals. They had first come to national notice at the Brighton assembly in 1966, where they were branded as the Red Guards and championed left-wing causes like worker co-operatives and withdrawing from NATO. There was no fashionable progressive issue of the time which escaped encapsulation in a slogan on a Young Liberal badge. 'Make love not war' was one of the favourites.

The Young Liberals played a large role in the student upheavals of the late 1960s. To the alarm of older Liberals, they frequently worked in alliance with the Young Communists. They professed a philosophy of liberation, which they applied to Vietnamese peasants, black South Africans, workers and students alike. They were a frequent irritant to the Liberal leadership, but they could not be ignored. In 1967, for instance, there were almost as many delegates at the Young Liberal conference as there were at the party's main annual assembly.

Jeremy Thorpe was particularly impatient with the YLs. The constant friction between the leadership and the youth movement reinforced the charge that the party's ideas lacked coherence. The issue which caused the most trouble was that of Palestine. The Young Liberals, particularly Louis Eaks, who became chair in 1968, were strongly pro-Palestinian. Many of the party's old guard had strong sympathies with Israel. More crucially, some of the Liberals' most important financial backers took that view. When Tony Greaves defeated Eaks for the chair in 1969, he was summoned by Jeremy Thorpe and told to get the policy changed. He protested that it had been agreed democratically, and that he could not alter it.

There were threats that the Young Liberals might be expelled en bloc from the party. A commission was set up to investigate their relationship with the party, but it ended up recommending only that local parties should have the right to reject as full members those who had joined the youth movement.

There were efforts by both sides to heal the breach. One of the young activists of the period, Stuart Mole, remembers Thorpe appearing for the cameras in front of a wall bearing a Young Liberal slogan reading 'To hell with politicians'. The problem was that in his three-piece suit he could not help looking a quintessential part of the political establishment.

The Young Liberals may have deterred centrist voters from supporting the party, particularly through the activities of the 'Stop the Seventy Tour' campaign, led by the then YL Chairman Peter Hain. Although the party was united in its abhorrence of apartheid, the militant direct action around rugby and cricket grounds which the campaign favoured antagonised many people. On the other hand, the Young Liberals were extremely energetic. They threw themselves into leafleting and canvassing, and were to form the core of the activists who developed community politics so successfully in the early 1970s. While some of the more militant leaders of the YLs, like George Kiloh and

Terry Lacey, ended up in the Labour Party, others, like Tony Greaves and Gordon Lishman, have remained active Liberals and Liberal Democrats. Stuart Mole was close to joining the Labour Party too, but Peter Hain dissuaded him. Hain himself defected to Labour in 1977.

The other significant development was the passing of David Steel's private member's bill to liberalise abortion. The bill established David Steel, who was still under thirty years old, as a considerable political figure on the national stage. It also identified the importance of the Liberal Party in the social revolution of the 1960s, which extended to homosexual law reform and the abolition of capital punishment, as well as to abortion. Most importantly, it was a lesson in the potential for cross-party co-operation. It forged the first links between David Steel and the then Home Secretary Roy Jenkins, although David Steel says that he only got to know Jenkins well during the European referendum campaign.

One of Jeremy Thorpe's greater strengths was as an organiser. He was able to put the party on a slightly sounder financial footing and to make the organisation marginally more professional. None of this was enough to prevent a great setback at the 1970 election. With Labour and the Conservatives neck and neck, the Liberals were squeezed. The share of the vote went down from 8.5% to 7.4%. The party had briefly had thirteen MPs following Wallace Lawler's 1969 by-election in Birmingham Ladywood, a seat which disappeared in boundary changes. The personal loyalty which Lawler had built up against the national trend, initially by running a Tote scheme, did not transfer into the rest of a new constituency of which his original patch now formed only a part. But he was far from being the only casualty. The party was right back down to its 1950s level of six. Several of the MPs survived with minuscule majorities. Wipe-out was avoided by an alarmingly small margin. The combined majority of Jeremy Thorpe, John Pardoe and David Steel was only fifteen hundred.

The one more hopeful factor for the Liberals was that the Conservatives were in power again, and the Liberal Party always performed better during periods of Tory rule. With the reduction in parliamentary strength, the activities of the party in the country became steadily more important. Community politics was enshrined at the party's 1970 Eastbourne assembly, as a new strategy to help the party recover from the setback of that year's general election. The ideas came from the grass roots; Jeremy Thorpe and other leaders were initially suspicious of the approach. Its focus was on working within council wards, picking up issues of local concern and working with the community to try to solve them. Its mainstay was cheap offset litho technology and the production of prodigious numbers of leaflets.

The resolution passed at Eastbourne talked about 'a dual approach to politics, acting both inside and outside the institutions of the political establishment ... to help organise people in their communities to take and use power ... to build a Liberal power-base in the major cities of this country ... to capture people's imagination as a credible political movement, with local roots and local successes'. The vote was 348 to 236. Opposition came from distrust of the more long-haired and exotically bearded Young Liberals, whose direct-action techniques were felt to have alienated voters. In truth, different people meant different things by community politics. At one end of the spectrum was the kind of local campaigning which had been successfully practised since Orpington, concentrating on practical issues like pedestrian crossings and broken paving stones. At the other end was a utopian aim for a revolutionary transformation of society.

The most purist of the community politicians held parliamentary politics in something close to contempt, and regarded the Parliamentary Liberal Party with the deepest suspicion. Their goal was to transform communities by empowering the people who lived there. Their focus, as well as their 'Focus' leaflets, was almost entirely directed towards the local council.

Community politics, practised by mostly young activists, attracted great criticism from the other parties. They charged that the Liberals were all things to all people; that policies in different parts of the country contradicted each other; and that people who were preoccupied with paving stones would have nothing to contribute to the Mother of Parliaments.

The fact remained, however, that community politics was highly successful. It began to yield results not only in the traditional rural areas but also in urban Britain. In 1973, the legendary Trevor Jones, 'Jones the Vote', won control of the city of Liverpool for the party with 48 of the 99 council seats. It was an astonishing performance in an area where the party had been written off completely until very recently. When Trevor Jones himself was first elected just five years before, in 1968, he was one of only two Liberal councillors.

The key to the success in Liverpool was the 'Focus' leaflet. It was first devised by the future Leader of the council, Cyril Carr, and his agent Alec Gerard in the run-up to the 1962 local elections. They decided that the traditional election address had limited appeal to voters. People were much more likely to read a local newsletter about issues which immediately concerned them. Originally called 'Church Ward News', the title was later changed to 'Focus'.

The concept was closely allied to the proposition that Liberals campaigned all year round, not just at election time. It was no good calling on somebody and just asking them to vote for you; you had first to establish that you were interested in their problems and prepared and able to do something about them. Soon Liberals in the rest of the city were following the 'Church Ward' lead. Trevor Jones became the chief proselytiser of the 'Focus' approach. He developed the leaflets, made them more populist and punchy and spearheaded their introduction into the rest of the country. He based his approach on elementary marketing principles. As far as possible, the leaflets would mention the names of individual roads. Jones knew that the most common complaints to the council were about cracked paving stones and fouling by dogs, so these concerns featured very strongly. Subsequently, he would borrow a line he had picked up from a Nelson Rockefeller campaign in New York and suggest in a leaflet that if all the paving stones his councillor wife Doreen had got fixed were laid end to end, they would reach from her ward to the Pier Head and back again. The greatest tribute to the 'Focus' approach is that it has now been adopted, with varying degrees of skill, by both the Labour and Conservative parties.

The Liberals were able to make a real difference in Liverpool. The ever-persuasive Sir Trevor dragooned Wimpey into helping to build the first low-cost houses for sale in an inner city area. When the first development of 298 houses went on the market, 3,000 people queued to try and buy one.

Elsewhere too, Liberal councillors were elected in large numbers, gained experience of power and became a major force within the party. Then, off the back of the successes at council level, the Liberals started winning by-elections. The first was at Rochdale. This was the seat which Ludovic Kennedy had come close to winning in the 1950s. The party's standard-bearer in October 1972 was the outsize local politician Alderman Cyril Smith, who was extremely well known in the constituency. Added to this advantage was considerable public dissatisfaction with the Heath Government and a feeling that the Labour Party was drifting too far to the left. *The Times* reported that 'it would be rash to assume that it means a Liberal revival but it does probably mean that centre party politics are becoming the trend at this point between general elections'.

The paper was much less equivocal about the next by-election gain, less than two months later, when the twenty-nine-year-old Vice-

Chairman of the Young Liberals, Graham Tope, won hitherto 'true blue' Sutton and Cheam with a majority of 7,417. 'No by-election upset since 1945', it said, 'compares in scale, or possibly significance, with what happened at Sutton and Cheam. To find comparison it would be necessary to go back to the Fulham by-election of 1934.'

Jeremy Thorpe called the victory 'a great Liberal breakthrough'. He predicted that 'by the time the next general election comes, this party is not only going to get back into the House of Commons, but it will be back in greater business than it has ever been for fifty years'.

The key to the Liberal success at Sutton lay in a northern import. Trevor Jones descended from Liverpool in his Triumph Stag to run the campaign. Jones regarded Sutton as a test-bed to see whether the techniques pioneered in Liverpool would transplant to other soils. He told Tope that if he did exactly what he was told, smiled when he was told to smile and scowled when he was told to scowl, Jones could make him an MP.

Sutton was deluged with 'Focus' leaflets, which had been printed in Liverpool. Previous Liberal leaflets had read like an edition of the *Guardian*; these felt more like the *Sun*. One particularly striking one, about road safety, featured a silhouette of a car turning into a skull with a headline 'Death Stalks the Crossroads'.

While Graham Tope, under Jones's tutelage, campaigned hard on local issues like road safety and concessionary bus fares for pensioners, party headquarters took an arm's-length approach to his efforts. As at Orpington, the Conservatives made the mistake of delaying the by-election for several months, but the Liberals left Jones and Tope largely to their own devices during the run-up period. There was suspicion of the community politics style and great scepticism as to whether the seat could be won. It was only in the closing two weeks, with polling evidence pointing to an upset, that the party threw all the resources at its disposal into Sutton.

On polling day, David Steel came to help with the final leaflets. Jones told him that victory was in the bag; he said everyone might as well go to the races for the day. But he pretended that he had to go and vote first, and pulled a dozen polling cards out of his pocket. It was all a big joke, but Jeremy Thorpe was sufficiently worried when he heard about it to ring Jones to make sure that he was not really planning to impersonate one or more Sutton voters.

The following July, the Liberals won two by-elections in previously safe Tory seats on the same day. The victories were won in very different ways. The candidate in the Isle of Ely was the gourmet and television personality Clement Freud. The party had not had a candidate here at all in 1970, and one of the keys to Freud's victory was the fact that he was a national celebrity. David Austick in Ripon was a completely different kind of candidate – a bookseller not known for his charisma, he was a classic hard-working local politician. After this historic twin victory, the Liberals again claimed that they were on the verge of a major breakthrough. Jeremy Thorpe said, 'The last time Liberals had victories on this sort of scale was in March 1929, when we won two seats from the Tories in the space of twenty-four hours.' He made a pledge to fight 500 seats at the next general election compared with the 332 fought in 1970.

The commentators were more sceptical. They felt that the results showed all the signs of a mid-term protest, albeit an unusually strong one. The big story of the by-elections, as far as they were concerned, was not so much the Liberals' success as the failure of the Labour Party to capitalise on the Government's problems.

There was a fifth by-election gain during the 1970–74 Parliament, when Alan Beith won Sir William Beveridge's old seat of Berwick-upon-Tweed. Although Berwick proved to be the most enduring of all the victories of the early 1970s, the result had less impact on the press at the time than those which had preceded it. The seat had become vacant after the Defence Minister Lord Lambton resigned over a relationship with a call-girl and a Liberal win had been forecast. In the event, the contest turned out to be much tighter than had been predicted; the Liberal majority on the night was only fifty-seven votes.

The party made progress on the same day in a by-election in the safe Tory stronghold of Hove. Des Wilson, a household name from his days of running the homeless charity Shelter, had been persuaded to stand for the Liberals by Trevor Jones. Although not wholly persuaded of the paving-stone approach, Wilson made a big impact with an uncompromisingly radical stance, and came within 4,000 votes of taking the seat.

Press comment again concentrated less on Liberal success than on the further failures of the Labour Party. *The Times* predicted that the Liberals would lack the resources and the candidates to fight convincingly on a broad front at the next general election. That proved to be an underestimate. In February 1974, the Liberals fielded over 550 candidates. The tally marked a dramatic advance over the previous fifteen years. In 1959, the party had put up only 216 standard-bearers, and there were around 150 constituencies in which there was no Liberal organisation at all; in many of them, there had been no Liberal candidate since the 1920s.

Nonetheless, there was no great expectation that the Liberals would achieve more than a modest advance in the February 1974 general election. Ted Heath had called it against the background of the miners' strike on the issue 'who governs?'. On balance, the betting was that the Conservatives would be returned.

The Liberals, despite the increase in the number of candidates, were ill equipped to fight a national campaign. Jeremy Thorpe, remembering the narrow squeak which he had experienced in 1970, decided to remain in North Devon. He held national press conferences from his headquarters in Barnstaple via a television link, which cost the party the large sum for that time of £16,000. The initiative had its advantages. It associated the Liberal Party with state-of-the-art technology, while at the same time cutting down the number of difficult questions which the press could ask. John Pardoe, who had charge of party organisation, took the decision to send the Director of Research down to Barnstaple for the duration of the campaign to make sure that the Leader stuck to party policy. Not everybody was happy with the arrangement. Campaigners like Trevor Jones complained that the cash that went on the TV link would have been better spent on literature for marginal seats.

Meanwhile, the election was beginning to unravel for the Conservatives. A story which later turned out to be inaccurate appeared in the *Daily Mirror* headlined 'The Great Pit Blunder', suggesting that the Pay Board had miscalculated the level of miners' pay against the rates paid to other manual workers. Miners were, the *Mirror* suggested, actually paid 8% below the national average. The inference was that the Government had been prevented from settling the pit dispute only by its own incompetence.

Furthermore, the Government was finding it difficult to concentrate the public's mind on the issue of 'who governs?'. Other issues became important which were far less helpful to the Conservatives and favoured the opposition parties.

The Liberals in particular benefited from their image as honest brokers seeking conciliation. The miners' strike, with the run-down of coal stocks, the introduction of the three-day week, the curtailment of television viewing and the exhortations to the public to clean their teeth in the dark, alienated people simultaneously from the Government and from the Labour Party, which was seen as too close to the unions. The Government appeared arrogant and incompetent at the same time, a fatal combination, but Labour commanded little confidence either. Whoever else was responsible for the mess, it was not the Liberal Party.

The 'b' word started to appear in the press. A week from polling day, the *Evening Standard* wrote, 'The Liberal Party is within sight of a permanent breakthrough.' The *Daily Express* in an editorial on 22 February 1974 raised the prospect of realignment: 'If there were a big switch from Labour to Liberal, a good number of moderate Labour members might then seek to create a new radical party by merging with the Liberals. The unions would then be in a position to bargain for favours with both parties.'

The polls were certainly producing some spectacular findings. Marplan recorded the biggest ever jump for a party during a general election campaign, with the Liberal rating of 12% on 10 February rising to 28% within a fortnight. The party's campaign committee predicted on 24 February that a minimum of sixty-four Liberal MPs would be elected.

The excitement grew as polling day approached. Thorpe's phenomenal self-confidence began to permeate the rest of the party. Cyril Smith called for one extra push in the next few days to produce 'a massive breakthrough'. After the Marplan poll for the ITV programme *Weekend World* put the Liberals on 28%, compared with 31.5% for Labour and 38.5% for the Conservatives Jeremy Thorpe, rated the most popular of the three leaders, started talking about the possibility of a Liberal overall majority: 'We are going for a landslide,' he said. This was to be the moment when the two-party system was ended for good.

On election night, the Liberals polled six million votes and over 19% of the national share. It was by far the party's strongest performance since the Second World War. The disappointment was that it yielded only fourteen seats. Three of the five by-election winners held on: Cyril Smith, Clement Freud and Alan Beith. Richard Wainwright and Michael Winstanley regained the seats which they had lost in 1970. Then there were also three first-time winners: Geraint Howells in Cardigan, Stephen Ross in the Isle of Wight and Paul Tyler in Bodmin.

Beyond the victories, there were many very impressive results. In Chelmsford, where a twenty-four-year-old Stuart Mole was the candidate, the vote share increased from 8% to 32%. Like the party's other strong showings, the achievement was based on hard work on the local council, aided by the complacency of the other parties. The party consoled itself with the hope that the next election would deliver a much better harvest of gains in seats like this.

Intriguingly, the national percentage share in February 1974 was very close to the Liberal Democrat vote in 2001, which yielded fifty-two MPs, almost four times as many. There are two big differences which explain the discrepancies between the two elections. The first is that there was less sense of targeting in 1974. Thorpe had made an effort to direct extra money to what were called 'special seats', but the computer-based techniques now used to focus messages to particular types of voter still lay far in the future. For the most part, candidates on the ground were just left to their own devices. In a campaign in which the Leader himself had stayed in his own constituency, there was little direction of any kind from the centre. Nevertheless, had the party known at the beginning of the campaign how successful they would be in terms of the national share of the vote, they could have concentrated their forces more effectively to increase the number of gains.

Secondly, there was little tradition in 1974 of tactical voting. Much of the effort in target seats by 2001 was directed at persuading Labour voters to switch to the Liberal Democrats to keep Conservatives out, and Conservatives to switch to the Liberal Democrats to keep Labour out. Modern campaigning tools were able to identify very clearly where the supporters of the third party in a constituency lived and to address the appropriate message to them.

The election result did give the fourteen Liberal MPs significant influence. No party had an overall majority. Although the Conservatives had fewer seats in the new Parliament than Labour, Edward Heath stayed in Downing Street and invited Jeremy Thorpe to discuss the possibility of coalition. There was a problem with Thorpe's telephone in Devon, and the message from Number 10 only got through at midnight on the Friday after the election.

By 4 p.m. on the Saturday, Jeremy Thorpe was in Downing Street for a hundred-minute discussion with Heath. Thorpe had not consulted any of his parliamentary colleagues before agreeing to see Heath; most of them heard about it on the radio. His justification was that if the Prime Minister asks to see you, you see him.

John Pardoe had advised Thorpe to tell the Prime Minister that he could not leave Barnstaple until after the weekend. He believed that if there were to be any talks, it was preferable that lieutenants on both sides should first prepare the ground. In any case, the talks were almost bound to prove abortive. Heath could offer Cabinet seats, but he could not offer any tangible progress towards proportional representation. Furthermore, even in combination with the Liberals, the Conservatives would still not have had an overall majority in the new House of Commons. Meanwhile, a cabal of the most senior Liberals, consisting of Jo Grimond, David Steel and Lord Byers, had met and was ready to persuade Jeremy Thorpe to turn Ted Heath's overtures down. After his meeting, Thorpe telephoned several senior colleagues. The message was overwhelmingly hostile to a deal. Trevor Jones for one told him, 'You might be in the Cabinet with a nice shiny black car, but the party will be somewhere else.'

There was great alarm in the Liberal Party at the faintest possibility of a coalition with the Tories. Jeremy Thorpe had appeared too eager for comfort to do a deal. Robert Carvel of the *Evening Standard* had described him arriving at Downing Street like 'a thirsty man going into a pub at opening time'. Peter Hain organised a petition amongst the party executive to reject coalition. John Pardoe echoed the widespread belief in the country that the Tories had lost the election and should cede office gracefully. He told his supporters in a meeting at Bude,

'When a British Prime Minister decides on a general election eighteen months before he needs to, to get a landslide mandate from the people on a purely spurious issue, and then they tell him to go and jump in the lake, then that man no longer deserves the confidence of anyone.'

Some believe that the mere fact that Jeremy Thorpe had gone to talk to Ted Heath damaged the party seven months later when the country went to the polls again. Labour supporters who might have voted tactically for the Liberals were put off because of the apparent closeness between Thorpe and Heath. It is impossible to tell whether this was true; it is clear, however, that if a deal had actually been done, without a copper-bottomed guarantee of proportional representation, it would have done enormous harm to the Liberal Party. It would have been unpopular with the electorate, which would have seen the Liberals as merely perpetuating the Government of a Prime Minister who had just lost an election. There would also inevitably have been a serious split in the party.

The truth was that a Con–Lib coalition at this stage could not possibly have worked. Even if he had wanted to do so, Ted Heath was not in a position to deliver proportional representation. Too many of his parliamentary colleagues would have dug their heels in. Shirley Williams recalls that the Labour party regarded the affair with restrained amusement.

As the dust settled, the Liberals came to believe that the disappointment over the tally of seats was only a temporary setback. Everybody knew that this Parliament would not last long. There was bound to be another general election soon. With 'one more heave', as the October general election slogan was rather unfortunately to become, the party could make the breakthrough which had so nearly happened in February. There was some independent support for this view. *The Economist* wrote on 9 March 1974, 'The size of the Liberal vote does indicate that a crisis in the two-party system has really arrived, and the injustice of the fact that the Liberals got only fourteen seats for six million votes suggests that a crisis in the electoral system could be approaching.'

The Liberals had all to play for between March and October. Their poll ratings remained buoyant. There was a genuine feeling that fourteen seats for six million votes was unfair. And distrust of the Labour left was matched by the recent memory of the mess which the Conservative Government had made of the miners' strike. A party which appealed to the centre and which called for co-operation instead of confrontation was an attractive proposition.

The other parties took the threat seriously. William Whitelaw, who was appointed Chairman of the Conservative Party in the summer, announced that his first task was to woo back former Tory supporters who had voted Liberal in February.

In July, the Liberals received a useful boost when the former Labour Defence Minister Christopher Mayhew crossed the floor to sit on the Liberal benches. There was speculation that more Labour MPs might follow, although none actually did. Jeremy Thorpe claimed that the party was at a watershed; the possibilities for the future were almost unlimited.

The polls showed the party at around 20%, with a narrow gap between the Conservatives and Labour. There was much talk in the press about the Liberals holding the balance of power in the next Parliament. Roger Carroll, the *Sun*'s Political Editor, wrote in June that if Jeremy Thorpe held the balance of power in the next Parliament, he could argue that the two-party system was dead. Peter Jenkins put the case in the *Guardian* for a Lab–Lib coalition after the next election. *The Times* talked of the possibility of Jeremy Thorpe being the first Liberal Leader to hold a Cabinet post for thirty years.

Some colleagues were very critical of Jeremy Thorpe at this time for not doing more to capitalise on the mood. At one point John Pardoe, who had been in general a great ally, threatened to stand for Leader against him. Then the new MP Paul Tyler came up with an idea. Given the near certainty of a second general election, he suggested a break with the tradition of abandoning politics for August. He had seen French politicians campaigning to good effect around the seaside resorts, and suggested that the Liberals should do the same.

Thorpe latched on to the proposal with great enthusiasm. To raise the profile of the tour, it was decided that he would travel by hovercraft. This kind of stunt was in Jeremy Thorpe's genes. His Conservative grandfather had once campaigned by balloon. The hovercraft tour was typical of the best and the worst of the Thorpe approach to politics. It was bold and original; it perpetuated the idea encouraged by the satellite-linked press conferences in February that the Liberals were fresh, innovative and comfortable with modern British technology. The tour was meticulously planned, down to the issue of yellow oilskins and wellington boots in appropriate sizes for those on board.

There was just one drawback. The first leg was to storm the beaches of the West Country. On the eve of the first day, John Pardoe asked Jeremy Thorpe what the message was. Thorpe said, 'I rely on you people.' The campaign from the start was long on dynamism but rather short on direction. Thorpe's landing on the beaches of Britain was impressive, but for all the Leader's powers of improvisation, he needed a bit more to say to the holidaymakers.

There was some predictable ridicule from opponents. The hovercraft was compared to the party: a hybrid which makes a lot of noise accompanied by a lot of useless spray. It could function solely in fine weather, another said, and could only skim the surface.

Nonetheless, the early part of the tour drew large crowds. A thousand people turned out to hear Jeremy Thorpe and his colleagues in St Ives. Another six hundred were there at Westward Ho!.

The grand plan had unfortunately not taken full account of the weather. It was a terrible summer, and the chosen form of transport was not equal to the seas. The first craft, christened *New Endeavour,* was damaged at Sidmouth. A second craft ran aground at Southport. The image was unfortunate for a party which was supposed to be going from strength to strength. The press had fun with images of MPs leaving the sinking ship. In retrospect, Jeremy Thorpe puts the vicissitudes of the tour down to bad luck, and he has a point. The first hovercraft had been used in the Middle East. Sand lodged in its rubber skirt had caused the accident. Furthermore, had the tour been timed for a week earlier, the weather would have been far better and all would have gone well.

By the end of the tour, the Liberals were developing a more coherent message. The biggest issue of the time was inflation. There was a sense of serious economic crisis, with genuine worry about the viability of the country's economy. The Liberals were the champions of a statutory prices and incomes policy. They claimed that the unions did not trust the Tories and the employers did not trust Labour. They were the only party which could appeal to both sides of industry.

As the date of a second 1974 election drew closer, the coalition question became ever more pressing. Under what terms would the Liberals contemplate a coalition? Would they be prepared to work with both the other parties, or only one? Inevitably, tensions within the party began to surface. The issue was very delicate. Whereas the Liberals leant more towards Labour than the Conservatives, Ted Heath's party was much more open to the idea of coalition than Harold Wilson's was. Meanwhile, the radicals in the Liberal Party were firmly attached to the idea of preserving its independence at all costs.

Jeremy Thorpe wanted to keep his options open. That led to a predictable diatribe from the Young Liberals. They put out a statement saying, 'We totally dissociate ourselves from anyone who puts personal power before Liberal aims and ideals. If Jeremy Thorpe continues to press for those forms of unsavoury political alliances, he will be left high and dry with the old Etonian flotsam and jetsam.' Thorpe and his accomplices, they said, would be traitors to the Liberal Party.

There was a great deal of tension ahead of the Liberal Assembly in Brighton. The dangers of a confrontation, which would have tied the hands of the leadership and damaged the image of the party, were considerable. In the event, both sides pulled back from the brink; the debate was a great deal more measured and civilised than had seemed likely. Nonetheless, it put clear limits on Thorpe's freedom to manoeuvre. His speech contained an important concession to his critics: 'We will fight this election', he said, 'on our own policies, under our own colours and with our own candidates.' When he went on to say 'we would be prepared for a limited period on an agreed programme to join an all-party Government of National Unity', there were some boos. Trevor Jones, often a critic of Thorpe, commented that 'national coalition means Liberal demolition'.

Thorpe had, however, at least left some options open without splitting the party down the middle. But at the same time as he was being required to tone down his enthusiasm for coalition, a somewhat desperate Conservative Party was moving in the opposite direction. By September, Ted Heath was promising to bring non-Conservatives into his Government even if he won an overall majority. So the Liberals no longer had a monopoly of the consensus-seeking vote.

The commentators went on taking the party's prospects very seriously. Peter Jenkins wrote, 'For the first time in post-war politics, it actually mattered, and mattered a great deal, what was decided yesterday at the Liberal Assembly.' Anthony Shrimsley told *Daily Mail* readers, 'Never in the colourful career of Jeremy Thorpe has he been so close to real power.'

The Liberals began the October election campaign in high spirits. They did not experience the dip in the polls which had characterised the first week of the February campaign. Thorpe's language was very upbeat.

He talked about making a total breakthrough and ending the two-party system. He said on the BBC TV programme *Midweek*, 'If the Liberals got nine million votes, we might get two hundred seats.'

Thorpe's enthusiasm started to run away with him. In the first week of the campaign, he promised that there was to be a prominent Labour defector from the House of Lords. The journalists were kept in suspense at the morning press conference; they were not told the name. Frantic calls were made to all the possible suspects from the Labour benches in the Upper House. When the new recruit was finally identified, there was a great feeling of anti-climax. It was Earl St Davids, a hereditary peer who had never held office and of whom very few people had even heard. Even the disclosure of his full name, Jestyn Reginald Austen Plantagenet Phillips, somehow failed to add gravitas.

Now defending a majority of over 11,000 instead of the three-figure margin of February, Jeremy Thorpe made an extensive national tour, largely by helicopter. He continued to receive a good press. There was still considerable speculation about what the Liberals would do if they held the balance of power. But somehow the party remained stuck in the polls.

When the results were announced, they were a bitter disappointment. Labour had a clear majority and the Liberal vote was actually down by 1%. Taking into account the fact that the party was fighting a hundred more seats than in February, the real drop was greater, 3% on average in the seats contested at both elections. The party had a net loss of seats as well. Paul Tyler and Michael Winstanley were out. Christopher Mayhew had decamped to Bath, but proved unable to overturn the Tory majority there. The one consolation was the arrival in the Commons of a larger-than-life Cornishman called David Penhaligon as MP for Truro.

'Bitter Thorpe faces another false dawn,' crowed the *Telegraph* headline. 'The day a Liberal dream crumbled,' said the *Mail*. 'Night when Jeremy's dreams of power died,' added the *Sun*. Their pictures of

Jeremy Thorpe suggested a man who was indeed despondent. Nobody knew at that stage that there might have been personal as well as political reasons for him to feel that way.

There are many possible explanations for the setback. It is quite conceivable that the Liberals frightened the voters back to the other parties by painting such a bleak picture of the economic situation. The Liberal solution – statutory wage and price restraint following a total freeze – was one which many people thought would damage their own pockets. Alternatively, in a national crisis, voters may not have felt willing to risk entrusting power to a party which was perceived to be so inexperienced. The *Times* reporter Christopher Walker had written during the campaign about the doubts in many voters' minds 'as to whether patently nice people like the Liberals are capable of handling the national crisis they talk about so often'.

Thorpe himself came under attack. His hovercraft tour had allowed the press to depict him as a somewhat accident-prone lightweight. During the election, journalists sought to perpetuate this image with descriptions of his helicopter forays and his penchant for leaping over rural five-bar gates. Butler and Kavanagh say in their Nuffield study of the October 1974 election that 'the image left by much of the coverage of Mr Thorpe was of an attractive clown rather than the carrier of a great Liberal message, let alone a father-figure who had an answer to the nation's problems'. Yet Thorpe was still a far greater asset to the Liberals than Heath was to the Conservatives. Asked which Leader had most impressed them, 14% told NOP that it was Heath, 27% Thorpe and 33% Wilson.

The Liberals' problem was their party as much as their Leader. The Liberals of the early 1970s were certainly not as cohesive as the Liberal Democrats are now. Many of the MPs were 'local heroes' – people who could legitimately claim to have been elected not because they were Liberals but because they were outsize personalities in the area.

Disagreements in the much smaller parliamentary party of those days were much sharper than the arguments of today, and the various organs of the party in the country could appear near-shambolic. The Liberals were sometimes fortunate that they did not receive as much press attention as their rivals did.

Jeremy Thorpe's target seems to have wavered during the campaign. He spent the first week attacking the Labour Government. He might have done better to have concentrated his assault on both the other parties consistently, drawing particular attention to the weaknesses in the Tories' economic policies.

Organisationally, the party was certainly weaker than the Liberal Democrats are today. Fighting two general elections in a single year was a huge strain on an organisation which was constantly short of funds. Targeting techniques had had no time to advance since the February election. And there was a problem over the clarity of the message. The feuding over the coalition issue, although it never came to a head, cannot have impressed floating voters. Most of all, however, the Liberals were simply subjected to the old two-party squeeze. It is doubtful that they could have done a great deal more to stave it off.

The *Sunday People* published a horoscope for Jeremy Thorpe at the end of 1974. 'Fun-loving Jeremy Thorpe', it predicted, 'will see his political stock erode in the next three years and possibly enjoy fame in his original profession, the law.' The clairvoyant was spot-on, although not perhaps in the way he intended.

4   The Pact, 1974–9

The years between 1974 and 1980 were troubled ones for the Liberal Party. There was none of the excitement of the by-elections of the early 1970s or of the near breakthroughs at the February and October 1974 general elections. Far worse, the party Leader was engulfed in one of the most sensational political scandals of the twentieth century.

There were fierce disputes between the activists throughout this period. The parliamentary party was also at its most fractious. The MPs had to cope with a double disappointment: it was not just the fact that there were fewer of them when they had so firmly expected there to be more; there was also the realisation that their influence was much less because the Government had a proper working majority. They had lost the leverage which they enjoyed during the brief period of the February 1974 Parliament.

Furthermore, there was a Labour Government, and the old pattern was reasserting itself, with the Liberals, having done well against an unpopular Tory Government, now performing poorly against an unpopular Labour one. At times, once again, there were to be serious questions about the survival of the party itself. It was a time for retrenchment and held nerves.

For all the vicissitudes and setbacks of this period, however, there were two developments of great importance to the future of the Liberal Party.

Neither should count, strictly, as breakthroughs, but both were of great importance to the development of the Alliance and the high expectations of the following decade.

The first of these developments was the referendum on the Common Market in 1975. Harold Wilson's Government had returned to power with a promise to renegotiate the terms of British membership of the EEC. If the Government deemed the renegotiation a success, there was a promise that the final judgement whether Britain should remain in the Community or not should be left to the electorate. Wilson duly declared that the renegotiation had been satisfactory, and the referendum campaign was set in train.

The significance to the Liberal Party was that the pro- and anti-Common Market camps cut across party lines. At the head of the pro campaign was the triumvirate of Roy Jenkins, Willie Whitelaw and David Steel. As the only party in which there was no serious division of opinion, the Liberals were to punch above their weight in the referendum battle.

Furthermore, the campaign forged new alliances across party boundaries. In the 1970s, parties were more tribal even than they are now. Politicians of rival parties rarely mixed with each other. David Steel says that he only came to know Roy Jenkins well when they fought this campaign together. The referendum may not have broken the mould of British politics, but at least it suggested that there were other possible moulds worth considering. Roy Jenkins observed afterwards that the campaign made 'some of the divisions in politics seem a little artificial'.

Equally, the campaign deepened the rift in the Labour Party between pro-market right and anti-market left. Harold Wilson had introduced the novel concept of suspending collective Cabinet responsibility on the issue of Europe. It meant that the infighting which is endemic to all Cabinets became much more overt. At one point in the campaign, Roy Jenkins said of his Cabinet colleague Tony Benn, 'I find it increasingly difficult to take Mr Benn seriously as an economics Minister.' At the same time, it was clear that Roy Jenkins was increasingly prepared to take David Steel very seriously indeed.

The referendum campaign began with polls showing a two-to-one split in favour of leaving the European Community. The eventual vote went almost exactly the other way, with two-to-one in favour of staying in. All kinds of arguments were put by each side. The choice, however, was mainly decided by a single factor. The sensible-looking people were on one side of the argument, and the mad-looking people were on the other. It did the Liberal Party no harm to be so firmly allied with the forces of sanity. It was not a quality which had always been associated with their cause.

Another strange experience for the Liberal participants on the pro-Market side was to be fighting a campaign that was extremely well funded by the business community. Helicopters and private jets could be conjured up to whisk them from rally to rally, no expense spared. There were lavish headquarters in Whitehall and off Park Lane. Archy Kirkwood, who was running the youth campaign, was asked what equipment he needed and suggested that some typewriters would come in handy. The next day six brand new state-of-the-art IBM typewriters arrived, still in their boxes. For somebody used to the ways of the Liberal Party, this was astonishing. As soon as the referendum was over, the Liberals had to put their old hair shirts back on, and resume their former hand-to-mouth existence. But they had had a taste of how the other half lived.

The Liberals were at least used to fighting their battles with hugely inadequate resources. The problem which engulfed the party in 1976 was of a totally different order. The extraordinary saga of Norman Scott, his shot dog and the allegations against Jeremy Thorpe came to dominate the press. David Steel and Emlyn Hooson had met Scott as early as 1971, heard his allegations of having a homosexual relationship with Thorpe and discovered that the former MP for Bodmin, Peter Bessell, had been paying him regular sums of money. They instigated a brief inquiry, which they conducted together with Frank Byers, listened to Thorpe's emphatic denials and, given the lack of conclusive evidence, let the matter drop.

The issue resurfaced during two sets of legal proceedings at the beginning of 1976. One concerned the shooting of Scott's dog Rinka. A man named Andrew Newton was charged with illegal possession of a firearm with intention to endanger life. The other was a charge against Scott himself for defrauding the Post Office; during the hearing in Barnstaple Magistrates' Court, Scott repeated his allegations about Thorpe, and journalists were free to write about them under the protection provided by the rules of court reporting.

When the details of the original 1971 investigation were disclosed to the parliamentary party, Bessell, who was now living in the USA, covered up for Thorpe by claiming that he had made the payments because Scott was blackmailing him.

Colleagues first stood by their Leader, then began to lose faith in him. The revelation that a close friend of Thorpe's called David Holmes had paid £2,500 to buy Scott's letters from Bessell began to undermine their faith in the Leader. Then it emerged that Holmes had been receiving large sums of money out of funds supposedly donated for elections. In no doubt about the disquiet amongst his colleagues, Thorpe declared himself prepared to submit to a fresh leadership election in the autumn. Most of the MPs, however, including previously firm supporters like David Steel, were now advising him to stand down forthwith. The affair was having a catastrophic effect on the standing of the party in the country.

Things went from bad to worse. Newton was sentenced to two years' imprisonment. No connection had been established with Thorpe or any other Liberals, but speculation was rife. Then Bessell claimed he had lied to protect Thorpe. Next, the *Sunday Times* published a letter from Thorpe to Scott containing the line 'Bunnies can (and will) go to France'. Then Richard Wainwright, never a strong Thorpe supporter, challenged the Leader to issue a writ for defamation against Scott.

Finally, Thorpe agreed to step down. But that did not end the agony for the party. In October 1977, Newton was released from jail to claim that he had been hired to kill Scott. In August 1978, Thorpe and three others were charged with conspiracy to murder, and Thorpe additionally with incitement to murder. The next month, Thorpe, who was on bail, insisted on appearing on the platform at the Southport Liberal Assembly, thereby guaranteeing that the press would have no interest in covering any other story from the week. The defendants were committed for trial at the Old Bailey just before Christmas 1978. The trial finally took place just after the 1979 election, and all four were acquitted.

The chain of events was disastrous for the Liberal Party, and put enormous strain on those who were trying to keep the show on the road. They were sustained by bouts of black humour. When it emerged in court that Newton originally searched for Scott in Dunstable instead of Barnstaple, David Penhaligon told his colleagues that this was the moment when he realised that there must be something in the story. It sounded all too typical of the kind of cock-up that characterised the Liberal Party.

As the Thorpe saga unfolded in 1976, the party was in the process of devising a new system for electing a leader. The previous contest in 1967 had shown the weakness of confining the choice to MPs by producing a stalemate. There was a great appetite for widening the franchise to party members. This being the Liberal Party, there were endless deliberations about the fairest possible system, which ended up with a fiendishly complicated formula for weighting votes according to the strengths of different constituencies. And this being the Liberal Party, the new system was not ready and agreed when a vacancy arose.

The solution was an interregnum. Jo Grimond, now very much an elder statesman, filled the breach. Many in the party wished that he had never stepped down in the first place. The old panache, humour and intellectual curiosity remained undimmed, even if the Leader's hearing had deteriorated further.

Eventually, a special conference was called in Manchester to finalise the new system for electing the Leader. Geoff Tordoff, the Chairman of the party, had a background in business and constructed a decision tree to follow through the consequences of the alternative courses of action. There was at least one route down which the party could go which would lead them to a complete impasse. Jo Grimond sought to reduce the tension with characteristic humour. He warned them to get on with it, because he was enjoying being Leader again.

Eventually, a new electoral system was agreed, combining nomination by the MPs with election by the membership. Two of the leading members of the parliamentary party duly stepped forward into the lists, David Steel and John Pardoe. They were old friends and the political differences between them were not fundamental. In the perennial debate about strategy, Steel leaned rather more towards co-operation with others; Pardoe sounded more protective of the party's independence. He did not believe that the Liberals could present themselves as a potential party of g overnment simply by allying themselves with more credibility on that score. He wanted the party to develop a much harder campaigning edge, championing causes like constitutional reform and decentralisation as a means of addressing Britain's economic failures.

Pardoe had not only been a member of the Labour Party but was also on its Bevanite wing. The press saw him as the champion of the Liberal left against Steel as the standard-bearer of the party establishment. They also branded Pardoe 'an effective bastard', while Steel's appeal was to the consensus approach. There were other differences between the two: Pardoe had more interest in policy, while Steel was a great tactician.

Steel's main preoccupations were with foreign affairs; Pardoe's with domestic issues like poverty and devolution.

The only serious rift between the two was over an issue of personal vanity. It was suggested to the parliamentary journalists that John Pardoe mysteriously seemed to have more hair than he used to have. Was he perhaps wearing a hairpiece? The story came from sources close to Steel who, it began to be said, was not as nice as he looked. Pardoe had earlier confided to Steel that he was taking steps to tackle his hair loss problem.

The Steel team believed that a bit of what they called 'Pardoe-baiting' might yield dividends. *The Times* reported at the time, 'Mr Steel's reference to the possibility that Mr Pardoe wore a hairpiece appears to have been genuinely meant as a joke, unlike much of the Pardoe baiting, but it put Mr Pardoe in a towering rage. If Mr Steel wins, he may be able to thank the Pardoe campaign.' At Pardoe's press conferences, photographers started to appear with small stepladders up which they climbed to take shots of what they considered to be the most newsworthy aspect of the candidate, the top of his head.

When the results were declared in Poplar Civic Hall, David Steel had won by considerably more than a short hair. He had 12,541 votes to Pardoe's 7,032. Steel's greatest asset was probably his higher profile. The Abortion Act in particular had meant that he was considerably better known than his rival was. Each of the three times the membership of the Liberal and then the Liberal Democrat parties have elected a leader, the candidate who was best known on television has won. The votes have been swung by the armchair members; if the activists alone were voting, the results would have been much harder to call. David Steel was also helped by an article in *The Times* which claimed that both Jeremy Thorpe and Jo Grimond, who were officially neutral, would be voting for Steel.

After the result, John Pardoe agreed to resume his role of economics spokesman. His chief henchman Cyril Smith also, after a brief sulk, resumed active Liberal service.

Nevertheless, Steel inherited a party in considerable trouble. The Thorpe affair was enormously damaging. Party members were demoralised, and poll ratings were poor. In this situation, David Steel's qualities were to prove invaluable. He was good at keeping his nerve. He was also infinitely patient and accommodating with the many independent and sometimes perverse figures of importance and self-importance in the party.

Most significant of all, he had a strategy. He believed that there was little point in having a Liberal Party at all if it did not aim for power. Given the current level of support and the number of parliamentarians on the Liberal benches, that inevitably meant working with other parties across the divide.

A policy of consensus with political opponents meant the risk of confrontation within the Liberal Party itself. David Steel's first Assembly as Leader was at Llandudno in September 1976. The Young Liberals threatened to demonstrate if he mentioned the word 'coalition' in his speech. Advisers tried to persuade him to tone down his remarks. He was, however, determined to start as he meant to go on.

The new Leader held several important cards. He was the first Leader to be elected by the entire membership. His margin of victory had been impressive. That meant that he had the authority to end the tensions between the party in the country and the party in Parliament. He was popular too with the press. There were great expectations of him. The Mayor, making his ritual welcoming speech at the start of the Llandudno Assembly, told the audience that they were on hallowed ground. This was the constituency which David Lloyd George had represented. And now a second David had come to redeem them.

David Steel left the most controversial part of his speech until near the end: 'If the political conditions are right,' he said, 'and if our own values are retained, we shall probably have – at least temporarily – to share power with somebody else to bring about the changes we seek.'

There was a demonstration from the radicals, who held up placards with the word 'No' on them. They had obtained a leak of the controversial passage by purloining the stencils on which the speech had been typed from a wastepaper basket. The demonstrators, however, were soon drowned out by the cheers of Steel's supporters. He went on:

> *I want the Liberal Party to be the fulcrum and centre of the next election argument – not something peripheral to it. If that is to happen we must not give the impression of being afraid to soil our hands with the responsibilities of sharing power.*
>
> *We must be bold enough to deploy the coalition case positively. We must go all out to attack the other parties for wanting power exclusively to themselves no matter how small a percentage of public support.*
>
> *If people want a more broadly based government, they must vote Liberal to get it. And if they vote Liberal, we must be ready to help to provide it.*

The opportunity for putting the theory into practice came sooner than anyone expected. The Labour Government was losing support fast. The Tories had a 16.5% lead in the polls. In early 1977, two previously rock-solid Labour seats, Walsall North and Workington, fell to the Conservatives, spelling the end of the Callaghan Government's overall majority. Labour were able to rely for a period on the support of eleven Scottish Nationalists and three Welsh Nationalists who wanted the Government's Devolution Bill to become law. The Government then, however, lost a timetable motion which meant that the Devolution Bill stood little chance of ever reaching the statute book.

It was only a matter of time before the Government lost an important vote. The crunch came in March 1977. The Government set plans before the Commons for spending cuts to the tune of £2,500 million, which the International Monetary Fund had demanded as the price of support for the beleaguered British economy. Labour lost a vote on a key clause and the Leader of the Opposition, Margaret Thatcher, duly tabled a motion of no confidence, to be debated six days later on 23 March.

There was only one way in which the Government could avoid a general election, a pact with the Liberals. David Steel was approached, via the respected Chairman of the Parliamentary Labour Party, Cledwyn Hughes. Steel made it clear that he would not be a pushover. He indicated that the party would be prepared for a general election if necessary, and indeed asked party headquarters to set the machinery for a campaign in train.

In a press release, Steel stipulated that Labour had a choice. Either they could sign up to a programme of agreed measures in the national interest, or there could be a general election. 'The one thing we cannot do', it went on, 'is stagger on with a lame duck Labour programme which has neither public not parliamentary support.'

The press nevertheless suggested that the Liberals were bluffing. So Steel upped the ante on the Saturday, making it clear that there would be thirteen Liberal votes against the Government unless there was an agreed programme. At this point, the contacts which David Steel had established during the referendum campaign came into play. He had a phone call from Bill Rodgers, the Transport Secretary, who undertook to pass on the terms which the Liberals were proposing to the Prime Minister. Rodgers in turn had been prompted by the journalist Peter Jenkins to make the approach.

David Steel's main demands were for direct elections to the European Parliament on the basis of proportional representation and progress on devolution for Scotland and Wales. The Liberals also wanted to block any further nationalisation and the more extreme socialist agenda of the Labour Party.

Callaghan was in fact to find the Liberals a very useful alibi in this respect in his battles against Tony Benn and the other left-wingers in his Cabinet. He frequently told his colleagues, 'As much as I would like to do this, I am afraid that the Liberals would not like it.'

Other conditions proposed by the Liberals were a little more difficult. Rodgers advised Steel that Callaghan could not guarantee to deliver proportional representation for Europe. They settled in the end for an agreement that the Government would give PR a fair wind. The other main provision was that there would be a formal consultative committee, giving the Liberals the right of consultation on Government legislation.

Steel was convinced that the pact would give the party a new relevance in British politics. There were a couple of doubters in the parliamentary party, Jo Grimond and David Penhaligon, but they decided to preserve unity and not to rock the boat. The party in the country were less sure about the move, but Steel knew he could command the considerable loyalty that he had won in the leadership election of the previous year. Geoff Tordoff organised a thorough consultation of the party through regional chairmen and key opinion-formers and was able to report back overwhelming support for the pact.

There was a good case for the pact to be argued in the country. It was to provide the consensus government which had been so lacking in the previous decade. It meant ruling out the socialist agenda of the Labour left. It gave Jim Callaghan, whose personal popularity was ahead of his Government's, some respite from the attacks to which he was being subjected in his own party.

David Steel believes that the main advantage of the pact was not so much in the details of policy which were implemented as in the impression which the country gained of the Liberal Party. At last, this was a party which mattered, which was responsible and which could make a difference to the Government of the country. The pact gave the Liberals a credibility which they had previously lacked. The weakness was that the Liberals were unable to capitalise on the fact that they had genuinely made a difference for the better. They never managed to earn the credit of the electorate for the achievements of the pact. This was a lesson well learnt by the Liberal Democrats, who entered partnership governments in Scotland and Wales in 1999.

There is no doubt that the pact did benefit the country considerably. The economy began to improve. Inflation came down: within six months of the pact's operation, it had been cut from 18% to 9.6%. The balance of payments went from deficit into surplus. Interest and mortgage rates were greatly reduced. Tony Benn was kept in check. His grand plans for restructuring the electricity industry into a single nationalised corporation were stymied. Towards the end of the pact's life, the Government introduced legislation to encourage profit-sharing, a longstanding Liberal policy. Direct elections were introduced for the European Parliament. The proposal that they should be by proportional representation was ultimately defeated, but Government ministers, including those like Michael Foot who were deeply opposed to the concept, did join the Liberals in the lobby in favour of PR.

There were, inevitably, hiccups. One early and serious one arose out of the Budget, which had been planned before the pact came into force but which took place afterwards. One provision was a five-and-a-half pence rise in petrol tax, a measure which appalled many Liberal MPs. The issue of petrol tax was to prove divisive again within the party in the late 1990s, with urban- and suburban-based environmentalists ranged against MPs with large rural constituencies, where the use of a car was essential. In 1977, almost all Liberal MPs represented rural seats, where the electoral consequences of supporting a hike in petrol tax were obvious.

John Pardoe had had a meeting with the Chancellor, Denis Healey, before Budget day at which Healey outlined the plan. In his speech in the Budget debate, nonetheless, Pardoe appeared to be hinting that the Liberals would vote to reduce the tax rise. The Government was furious, regarding this as a breach of the promise represented by the pact. James Callaghan made it clear that he regarded the issue as a vote of confidence.

David Steel dictated a press release leaving no doubt that the Liberals would after all support the Government. Then he telephoned his colleagues one by one to win them round. The pact narrowly avoided disintegration within a month of its birth. Later the government did in fact drop the increase in petrol tax.

Relationships between Government ministers and their Liberal opposite numbers varied considerably. James Callaghan had a great respect for David Steel. Denis Healey, on the other hand, held John Pardoe in contempt. The two had some legendary rows. Healey says in his autobiography *The Time of My Life* that he found it particularly difficult working with Pardoe: 'He was robust and intelligent enough, but sometimes I felt he was simply Denis Healey with no redeeming features. More than once Joel Barnett [the Chief Secretary to the Treasury] had to pick up the pieces after we had sent the crockery flying.' At one of their meetings over the Finance Bill, Callaghan insisted that David Steel and Joel Barnett went along as well. 'I think you and I are only there to hold the coats,' Barnett suggested to Steel.

Other relationships were chequered. Bill Rodgers says in his memoirs that he liked his opposite number David Penhaligon, but found his working methods disorderly. Alan Beith, however, established a very good relationship with his counterpart as Chief Whip Michael Cocks, which was to be of huge benefit to the party as the 1979 general election approached.

Shirley Williams believes that the Labour Party would never have gone very far to meet the Liberal agenda. At a Cabinet meeting in 1975, Roy Jenkins had proposed a package of reforms including a Speaker's

Conference on PR, freedom of information legislation and bringing the European Convention on Human Rights into British law. She had supported him, and Tony Benn had shown some sympathy for some of the legislation, but all the rest of the Cabinet was opposed.

Tom McNally, working at the time in Number 10 Downing Street, had the impression that the Liberals had less impact than they could have done during the pact, because the proposals which they made to the Government were too vague. In fairness, it has to be borne in mind that at this period the Liberal Party had very little research back-up. It was impossible for the tiny band of party staff to match the Civil Service machine on which the Government could rely.

The pact undoubtedly benefited the country. The period of Lib–Lab rule was a great deal better than the period of Labour-only government which had immediately preceded it. The advantages did not, however, translate into votes. The local elections of May 1977 were disastrous, with the Liberals losing three-quarters of their county council seats. The party, which never needed much incentive to become fractious, became exceedingly restive. By the Brighton Assembly of autumn 1977, David Steel knew that he would have to make a very robust defence of the pact:

> We will enter the next election not just as a party equipped with splendid policy pamphlets and an excellent history in government in the distant past, but as a party which has shown itself not afraid to roll up its sleeves and dirty its hands with some responsibility for the direction of national policy, and then made a good job of it. As Shakespeare's Henry V said on the eve of the battle of Agincourt, 'He that hath no stomach for this fight, let him depart.'

There was one Liberal MP, well known for the size of his stomach, who had indeed been voicing doubts about the pact. Cyril Smith was incensed by the reference, and went around accusing David Steel of making cheap and wounding personal remarks about him. Steel duly denied that any personal reference had been intended in his Shakespearean quote.

Earlier in the summer, David Steel had persuaded his parliamentary colleagues to renew the pact for the coming parliamentary session. At a meeting in June, the MPs produced a ten-point plan outlining a series of rather vague priorities to which James Callaghan had no difficulty in signing up. By July, Steel had the endorsement of his parliamentary party for renewal, supported by some more enthusiastically than others. The Leader followed this up at Brighton by securing a two-to-one majority against those calling for the agreement to be renegotiated. There had, however, been an amendment passed which spelt out the need for Labour MPs to support PR for Europe by a substantial majority as a condition for continuing the pact.

The vote on the PR issue in the House of Commons eventually took place on 13 December 1977. Government ministers and a bare majority of Labour MPs supported PR, but the combination of the Tory opposition and a large minority from the Labour benches saw the measure defeated by eighty-seven votes.

It was a low point for David Steel. PR was the great prize which had eluded the Liberals for so long. Once it had been established for European elections, it was felt, it would have become much easier to get rid of 'first past the post' for Westminster. It was with this hope that so many queasy Liberals had agreed to support the pact.

On the other hand, PR for Europe was not a cause which would have garnered many extra votes for the party at a general election. Neither the European issue nor electoral reform had much resonance with the voters. Instead, they would have blamed the Liberals for forcing an unnecessary general election campaign on the country.

David Steel pointed out to his parliamentary colleagues that Labour had fulfilled their side of the bargain. The Government had voted for PR and a majority of Labour MPs had supported it. Much of the Liberal

Party, however, was in revolt. John Pardoe and Cyril Smith had gone on the airwaves denouncing the Labour MPs who had thwarted the Liberal dream. Telegrams and phone calls were pouring in from party members demanding an end to the pact. The Chairman and the President of the Party, Geoff Tordoff and Gruffyd Evans, went to David Steel's home in Ettrick Bridge to tell him that he could no longer carry the party. The MPs were badly split, but Steel was determined to soldier on. Ultimately, a provision was invoked which the Liberal Party Council, an unpredictably body dominated by activist zealots, had devised the previous month. There was to be a special Liberal assembly.

This gathering duly took place in Blackpool on 21 January 1978. With Cyril Smith leading the opposition to him, Steel won the day by 1,727 to 520. He used up a great deal of political capital in the process. The clinching arguments were that he would resign if he lost and that in any case the pact was only due to last until July. He attacked the party for its faint-hearted attitude to the pact:

> *If opinion polls show people believe that the pact is good for the country, but that they are not prepared to vote Liberal, the fault must be with the party. Our fault – yours and mine – but the potential is there.*
>
> *We will never project this agreement if we are apologetic and defensive about it. We have to be aggressive and positive. We will never project it to the electorate until the party workers themselves are convinced we are on the right course.*
>
> *I look forward to obtaining the balance of power at the next election, putting the thumbscrews on the next Government and opening the door to the introduction of more Liberal policies.*

So David Steel had his way and the pact duly ended in an orderly fashion in July 1978, after new Devolution Bills for Scotland and Wales had been passed. That autumn, there was a widespread assumption that James Callaghan would call a general election. He let it be known during the Labour Party Conference that he would be making a special ministerial broadcast. Everybody believed that this would be the moment for firing the starting gun. Instead, to the astonishment of all, he announced that he intended to soldier on into the following year.

The decision deprived the Liberals of yet another potential breakthrough. If Callaghan had gone to the country in autumn 1978, the polls suggested that the result would have been a hung Parliament. The Liberals could have claimed the credit for the improvement in the country's economy which had taken place during the period of the pact. They might easily then have gone into government with Labour. Margaret Thatcher might never have become Prime Minister.

Instead, Callaghan soldiered on into the Winter of Discontent. Labour's unpopularity grew markedly as rubbish piled up in the streets and the dead lay unburied. And the Liberals found themselves shouldering much of the blame, even though most of the mistakes had been made after they had ended the pact.

David Steel went into the 1979 general election campaign with his back to the wall. It was, as he remembers, a survival election. Potentially, it could have been a rerun of 1970 or worse. One poll put the party's support at only 5%. The *Sunday Express* predicted that one sole Liberal MP, Jo Grimond, would be returned in the new Parliament.

There was one ray of sunlight. Right at the end of the Parliament, a vacancy arose in the seat of Liverpool Edge Hill. There was some doubt whether a by-election would be held, or whether the vacancy would simply be left until a general election, which could not be far away. Here, the good relationship that Alan Beith had established with Michael Cocks played a critical role. Cocks, who strongly disliked the left-wingers who dominated the Liverpool Labour Party, made sure that the writ was moved for the by-election in the nick of time.

If the Liberals had been offered a choice of any seat in the country which they liked to fight a by-election, they would have probably chosen Edge Hill. They held all but one of the council seats there, and had adopted as prospective candidate David Alton, a young Liverpool councillor, who was Deputy Leader to Trevor Jones.

Right at the end of the Edge Hill campaign, the Government fell. The MPs who were lined up to appear at the eve-of-poll rally all cancelled to rush back to London for the vote of no confidence. One of their number, Clement Freud, had a private member's bill on freedom of Information on the stocks. The Government offered to give him support if he contrived to miss his train back from Liverpool. He resisted temptation and caught the train.

The Government was duly defeated, and the following day Alton won the by-election by a landslide. He had just enough time to make his maiden speech before having to fight the seat all over again, but his election, the first by-election gain for six years, was a powerful morale-booster to a beleaguered party. It may well have saved it from disaster at the general election. The Liberals' ratings in the national polls doubled overnight.

The party had one other enormously important asset in the personality of David Steel. This was the only one of the three general elections he fought as leader when he had total charge of the strategy; in both 1983 and 1987 he was in double harness with the SDP. It was one of the best campaigns that the party had ever fought. Steel became the first leader of any party to campaign in a general election by 'battle bus'. He copied the idea from the Conservative by-election campaign which had elected Sir Alec Douglas-Home in the Perth and Kinross by-election of 1963. The Steel bus, however, had sophisticated technology on board, including radio telephones. Since the tragic death of the Tory MP Airey Neave at the hands of the IRA, all political leaders had been given heavy police protection. The Liberals found this of great assistance in getting through heavy traffic.

Aboard the bus, David Steel took his message of consensus and co-operation the length and breadth of the country, and slowly the Liberal percentage began to creep up in the polls. The party ended up with 14% and eleven MPs, including David Alton. Compared with the prospects at the beginning of the campaign, this was a miracle. The casualties numbered, however, three of the party's most senior MPs. The loss of Jeremy Thorpe, who was preparing to stand trial, was predictable. The defeats of John Pardoe and Emlyn Hooson were a considerable blow.

John Pardoe believes that he lost because of a sense of let down after he had failed to be elected Leader in 1976. He found it harder to persuade local members to work actively after David Steel's victory. Others would point to the fact that Pardoe's seat was next door to Jeremy Thorpe's, and that he could not escape the negative publicity which the Thorpe saga had been attracting to the party for so long. Pardoe does not blame the pact for his seat loss, but he does nevertheless feel that it was a mistake: 'If I had been Leader, the pact would never have happened for the simple reason that you cannot put the Liberal Party's head in a noose unless you are absolutely sure that you have PR in your grasp.' He believes that David Steel was determined to make the pact work at the expense of achieving anything which the Liberals could claim as a tangible gain for their policies. It simply gave the impression, he thinks, that Liberal MPs would do anything to save their seats.

David Steel, unsurprisingly, differs. He believes that the pact gave the party a much higher media profile than it otherwise would have had. It also demonstrated that the Liberals were capable of wielding real influence.

The question remains whether the Liberals could have extracted more benefit from the pact. Was PR, at least for Europe, ever really within their grasp? David Steel thinks that it just might have been, but he points out the enormous obstacles in its path. A large proportion of Labour MPs was firmly opposed both to PR and to Europe. Persuading them to vote against their consciences on one of these issues was possible; to induce them to do so on both was a very tall order.

There were, nonetheless, lessons to be learnt for the future. Although David Steel had outlined his attitude towards coalition at Llandudno, when a pact actually became a possibility, it almost seemed to take the party by surprise. By contrast, the Liberal Democrats and the Labour Party carefully negotiated joint plans for constitutional reform well ahead of the 1997 election. And when the Scottish and Welsh Liberal Democrats entered partnership government after 1999, they made sure that they drew up much more detailed lists of negotiating points than the Liberals had in 1977. Further experience meant an even more strongly defined negotiating stance when a new partnership was formed after the 2003 Scottish Parliament elections.

The pact also drew attention to the cumbersome decision-making processes within the Liberal Party. The behaviour of the activists during this period undoubtedly prejudiced some of the members of the newly formed SDP against their partners during the formation of the Alliance four years later. When the Liberal Democrat constitution was drawn up, great efforts were made to ensure a less anarchic system.

In the 1970s, it was difficult for the Liberals to argue that they were a major party on a par with Labour and the Conservatives. They had few parliamentary seats and their poll ratings were low. They had no MPs with any experience of office. That inevitably limited the clout which they had with the Government. On all these counts, the Liberal Democrats are far stronger today.

The Liberal Democrats have also had the advantage of never having to fight an election against a backdrop of a trial in which their immediate ex-Leader was charged with conspiracy to murder.

5 Breaking the Mould, 1979–83

Between 1960 and 1980, the Liberal Party had had a switchback ride. Each time it went up, it went up slightly higher than before. Each time it came down, it did not come down quite so low. But there was still an awfully long way to go. There were eternal optimists within the party's ranks who worked ferociously hard in the belief that sooner or later the cause of righteousness would triumph. There were a few who secretly quite liked the party the way it was. The last thing they wanted was power and responsibility. If that had attracted them, they would have joined one of the other parties.

Both camps would gather for the regular tribal singsongs at the Glee Club at the party assembly, where one of the favourites was 'Losing Deposits'. This was sung to the tune of 'Waltzing Matilda'– as in 'Who'll come a-losing deposits with me?' When they got bored with that, they would retreat back to anthems of the far-off days when the party really was in power like 'The Land'.

Even with relatively low levels of support, the party had a role to play in the nation's affairs. At best, it provided a clear, though sometimes lonely, voice of conscience. It boasted battle honours for campaigns of great valour and worth: against Suez; for devolution; for British membership of the Common Market; for decency towards the Kenya Asians and Britain's ethnic minorities; for fair votes; for partnership in industry. It had done much good work in local communities as well. Liberal councillors consulted their electors a great deal more than others and, on the whole, worked harder for them as well. The party has never had safe seats at any level of government; its elected representatives have to be good to survive. A kind of political Darwinism comes into play.

Some Liberals, however, were not content to remain merely local champions or national voices of conscience. They believed that the only real point of politics was to gain national power. They knew that, however hard-working and able the party's activists and standard-bearers might be, it would take them for ever to get into government on their own. The only route to power had to lie through realignment in British politics.

At last, as 1979 and then 1980 progressed, that realignment began to look like first a possibility and then a probability. The Labour Party, having lost the general election, went on to lose its collective marbles. It had gone down to defeat because voters believed that the unions and the left of the party were wielding too much power. So the party responded by allowing the unions and the left of the party more power still.

A Trotskyite organisation known as the Militant Tendency had begun to infiltrate Labour's ranks. Its tactics were to gain control of local Labour parties by keeping meetings going until all the non-fanatics could not stand any more. Then votes would be taken to confirm the most hard-line positions and to elect the most hard-line people into office. The aggressive behaviour of the Militants and their unpleasantness towards those not of their persuasion meant that most normal people were driven away from Labour Party meetings at which they were present.

The Militant Tendency was only part of the problem. Other left-wingers who could not be described as entryists were determined to turn Labour into a genuinely socialist party. Tony Benn, who had been on a personal leftward march for many years, became their standard-bearer.

In policy terms, he wanted widespread nationalisation, unilateral disarmament and withdrawal from the European Community.

Those aims were matched by equally ambitious ones for the reform of the Labour Party, the purpose of which was to make sure that the leadership could not, as the Bennites saw it, betray the membership and the working class again. The main changes which they wanted were mandatory reselection for all Labour MPs, a new system for electing the party leader which involved constituency activists rather than just the MPs, and control of the manifesto. This was a programme which had deep constitutional consequences. Its effect was to subordinate elected representatives to the will of the party.

Most of the party's leading moderates had spent five gruelling years in Government. The assault from the left caught them when they were already dispirited and exhausted. Increasingly, divisions began to appear within their ranks. Some put their faith in the old-style solutions of the Labour right, which relied on making the occasional compromise while stitching up the votes which really mattered with the help of the remaining right-wing unions in the proverbial smoke-filled rooms.

But there were others who believed that the left-wing campaign for Labour Democracy had to be combated with a campaign for genuine democracy in the party, based not on the vanguard of the proletariat but on 'one member, one vote'. These were the leaders who were to form the nucleus of the new party, the SDP.

For some time, they had been fighting their corner on the key issues of policy. In May 1980, the party held a special conference at Wembley to approve a left-wing policy statement called 'Peace, Jobs, Freedom'. As Labour conferences had increasingly become, this was an opportunity for the left to heap vitriol on the right. The camaraderie of the nascent SDP was forged under Trotskyite fire of this kind. Sometimes, there was an opportunity to retaliate. In the defence debate at Wembley, struggling to be heard, the former Foreign Secretary David Owen tried to explain some home truths to the unilateralists: 'If you think you enter into arms control negotiations with your hands tied behind your back, with no form of leverage, you are deluding yourselves.'

Two other members of Jim Callaghan's Cabinet also despaired of the tack which the Labour Party was taking: Bill Rodgers, the former Transport Secretary who was MP for Stockton; and Shirley Williams, the former Education Secretary who had lost her seat at Hertford and Stevenage in 1979. With David Owen, they became known as the 'Gang of Three'. Their first joint statement concerned new Labour plans to call for withdrawal from the EEC. 'There are some of us', they said, 'who will not accept a choice between socialism and Europe. We will choose them both.' It was clear that they were actively considering a breakaway party.

Meanwhile, James Callaghan stood down, and Labour held its last leadership election under the old system, with only MPs voting. The victor was the old left-wing war-horse Michael Foot, who won by the tight margin of ten votes. He was backed by five Labour MPs who were later to join the SDP. They supported Foot in a deliberate attempt to marginalise and weaken the Labour Party, and to give the new party a better chance. Their role looks to have been decisive.

Speculation about new parties did not only centre round the Gang of Three. There was another part of the political jungle in which there lurked a very big beast indeed. Roy Jenkins had been Deputy Leader of the Labour Party under Harold Wilson. He resigned from the Shadow Cabinet after leading a large group of Labour rebels into the lobbies to support Ted Heath over joining the European Community. He returned to the front bench in 1974 as Home Secretary, then left Parliament in 1976 to become President of the European Commission. Even as early as that, he had hinted that he was considering a new political initiative. Choosing his language carefully, he told a farewell dinner that he did not intend ever to return as a Labour MP.

By 1979, as his term in Brussels drew to a close, Jenkins had become extremely detached from the Labour Party. That autumn he delivered the annual television Dimbleby lecture. His words clearly implied that he had in mind a new British political party. Twenty-four years on, it is striking how precisely he encapsulated the spirit of the philosophy which today's Liberal Democrats espouse, when he outlined the objectives of what he called 'the radical centre':

> *You make sure that the state knows its place, not only in relation to the economy, but in relation to the citizen. You are in favour of the right of dissent and the liberty of private conduct. You are against unnecessary centralisation and bureaucracy. You want to devolve decision-making wherever you sensibly can. You want parents in the school system, patients in the health service, residents in the neighbourhood, customers in both nationalised and private industry, to have as much say as possible. You want the nation to be self-confident and outward looking, rather than insular, xenophobic and suspicious. You want the class system to fade without being replaced either by an aggressive and intolerant proletarianism or by the dominance of the brash and selfish values of a 'get rich quick' society. You want the nation, without eschewing necessary controversy, to achieve a renewed sense of cohesion and purpose.*

At this stage, Roy Jenkins' ideas were not identical to those of the Gang of Three, who still talked in terms of socialism. Shirley Williams had stated her opposition to a centre party with 'no roots, no principles, no philosophy and no values'. The Gang of Three's idea of a new party was of the moderate type of social democracy to be found in many countries on the European continent. Roy Jenkins was much closer to being a Liberal.

Jenkins still had close supporters in the Parliamentary Labour Party. Robert Maclennan, a junior minister in the 1974–9 Government, was one of those who had come to doubt whether the old components of the Labour Party made sense any more for a radical reforming party. In addition to his reservations about the Bennites, he had experienced the bullying tactics of the trade unions at the Department of Prices and Consumer Protection, when Moss Evans of the Transport and General Workers' Union had tried to insist that the price of beer should be frozen. Then after the 1979 election, he saw the party espouse one position after another to which he was diametrically opposed. He wrote a letter to his constituency party saying that he would not stand again unless party policy changed. Privately, he decided to leave politics and take up a job in Hong Kong unless a new party could be formed.

Roy Jenkins was close to David Steel. There was much subsequent debate about whether Steel should have simply encouraged him and his supporters to join the Liberal Party. Many Liberals believe that it would have saved a great deal of the friction which existed between the two Alliance parties if this had happened. Cyril Smith summed up their view by saying at the time that the SDP should be strangled at birth.

But Steel himself took a different view. He thought that the dissident Labour MPs would make much more impact by forming a new party which then established a partnership with the Liberals. In retrospect, many believe that he was right. If the SDP had not been formed, it is very doubtful that all of the Gang of Three, if indeed any of them, would have joined the Liberal Party. David Owen's antipathy to the Liberals remains to this day. But at that time, Bill Rodgers and Shirley Williams were sceptical about them too. Furthermore, the SDP was to attract a large number of so-called political virgins, people who had never belonged to a political party before. Its supporters came from a remarkably wide variety of backgrounds, from ex-ambassadors and permanent secretaries to young couples from city council estates. It was very unlikely that the Liberal Party on its own would have had such a strong appeal.

Furthermore, although the existence of two parties created some logistical difficulties, it had its advantages. It embodied the philosophy of political co-operation which characterised the new politics that the two parties were preaching. It came across as something fresh and original in British politics.

The approach which David Steel and those close to him adopted was to mark the SDP as closely as possible. As one of them puts it, 'they couldn't have a piss without us being there'. The aim, rather than strangling them at birth, was to enfold them in the warmest and tightest possible embrace, so that the two parties became increasingly convergent, rather than divergent.

For all the tensions, the two parties did complement each other in very useful ways. The Liberals had more troops on the ground and more experience of campaigning as insurgents. They were used to fighting tough guerrilla battles against the larger, better-resourced parties. Most of the SDP's MPs had represented safe Labour seats; they had not needed to take to the streets in the relentless manner in which the Liberals had been schooled.

The SDP may have been short of infantry, but they had impressive generals, former senior Cabinet ministers who brought a new credibility to third-party politics. The Liberals had always had to deal with the criticism that they had no experience of Government. The last Liberal Cabinet minister had been Archibald Sinclair in 1945. Furthermore, the SDP brought excitement, innovation and commercial skills that were new to British politics. Here was a party which looked and sounded modern. There was a bold and distinctive logo. You could join by credit card. Its membership records were on computer, so that it could communicate properly with those who signed up. It had principles, but was not over-doctrinaire. Its leaders would have featured prominently in any journalist's list of the most media-friendly politicians. And the world's media were to flock to its launch.

That launch had become a certainty after another Labour special conference at Wembley in January 1981, called to sort out a shambles over reforming the system for electing the leader in a debate the previous autumn. Wembley approved an electoral college arrangement which the Gang of Three regarded as the final straw. The Parliamentary Party was to have only 30% of the vote, with 40% going to the trade unions and the other 30% to constituency parties.

The Gang of Three, together with Roy Jenkins, who had left Brussels a mere eighteen days before, met at David Owen's house in Limehouse on the day after Wembley, Sunday 25 January. There, having become a Gang of Four, they unveiled the 'Limehouse Declaration', a statement setting out the stall of a body which they called the Council for Social Democracy, supported by the signatures of a hundred luminaries. There was no doubt now that this was an embryo new party. Eight thousand messages of support came in the first week and a further 15,000 shortly afterwards. The momentum looked unstoppable, and the timetable was accelerated.

The SDP proper was duly launched in the Connaught Rooms in Covent Garden on 26 March 1981 in front of no fewer than 500 press. The Gang of Four then sped off to do a series of regional launches round the country. By covering two regions each, they established their presence in every part of Britain. The event potentially looked as significant as the launch of the Labour Party in 1900. Only this time, the new party was starting off with an overall lead in the polls. NOP for the *Observer* just before the launch gave the combination of the SDP and the Liberals 46%, Labour 27% and the Conservatives 25%. The Alliance as it was to beome was to go on to lead in the polls for six months.

The SDP promised to represent not just a new party, but a new approach to politics. As Roy Jenkins said in his speech at the launch, 'We want to get away from the politics of outdated dogmatism and the politics of class confrontation. We want to release the energies of people who are fed up with the old slanging match.'

The SDP could boast fourteen MPs at its launch, thirteen former

Labour members and one former Conservative, Christopher Brocklebank-Fowler. There were also eighteen peers and thirty-one former MPs. During the course of 1981, more and more Labour members joined. At one stage, there were twenty-nine MPs. At the outset, one of the most attractive features of the new party was its collective leadership. It added an extra dimension to the appearance of originality and freshness.

For a time, the SDP was sweeping everything before itself. When it was eventually halted in its tracks, the cause was an event which was totally unpredictable and completely outside its control, the Falklands War. That lay a year away. In the immediate aftermath of the launch, however, there were two very small clouds which had some bearing on the party's fortunes then, and which also carry lessons for the future.

First, the SDP was unable after Christopher Brocklebank-Fowler, or Chris Fowler as he started to become known, to recruit any more Conservative MPs. There were rumours about some big names, in particular the Employment Secretary Jim Prior, who had had some famous battles with Mrs Thatcher, but in truth there was little chance of snaring any of the Cabinet. Ian Gilmour, who was a friend of Roy Jenkins and philosophically closer to the SDP than to Margaret Thatcher, says that he was never tempted to join. A group of five backbench Tory MPs did come closer. One of them, Hugh Dykes, did much later join the Liberal Democrats. At that time, he was only prepared to cross the floor if his colleagues agreed to move with him, but none in the end was willing to take the plunge. On the other hand, the SDP's ranks did include some future Tory MPs, like Stephen Milligan and Gary Streeter.

Secondly, there was the issue of relations with the Liberal Party. It was agreed that there would be negotiations about which party should fight which seats. But it was inevitably a painful process, made worse by the mismatch in party organisation. The SDP's instinct was to do as much as possible at the centre. The Liberals wanted to give their constituency parties the maximum autonomy.

Furthermore, some in the SDP believed that it was the launch of their party that was making all the difference. They did not understand why the Liberals should have an equal number of seats. Many Liberal candidates felt the opposite: that they had put in a great deal of work on the ground in their constituencies and did not see why they should be expected to step aside. The negotiations were to drag on for months. One of the Liberal candidates most disappointed to be asked to step down for the SDP was Jim Wallace, who had been gearing up to fight Dumfries. He was not to know that his temporary misfortune was to pave the way for him to become the MP for the safest Liberal seat in the country, and later the first Liberal minister since the Second World War.

For the moment, however, the tensions lay well below the surface. As far as the public was aware, all was sweetness and light. The combination of success and a series of new challenges kept the two parties working very harmoniously together in the early months. Even the most cynical of the new SDP MPs, Neville Sandelson, could say that his new party was completely different from Labour because people stabbed each other in the back in such a nice friendly way in the SDP.

The first big challenge to the new party came as early as June 1981. Sir Tom Williams, the Labour MP for Warrington, resigned his seat to become a judge. It was a constituency where the Liberals had never had much of a presence. They had few party members and had won just 9% of the vote in the 1979 general election. The SDP had calculated that it was the 551st most winnable seat in the country. It was a hard decision for the new party to decide to fight the contest. Although Warrington was not at all fertile ground for the SDP, a poor result could have easily pricked the Social Democrat bubble. On the other hand, not to fight would have looked like cowardice.

The obvious choice of candidate was Shirley Williams. She was a politician with unparalleled charisma. Her personality would have appealed particularly to the Warrington electorate. She might conceivably have even won the seat. However, domestic circumstances were against her. Her brother had just died, and she was responsible for his two children as well as her own daughter. She felt that it was unfair to them to spend several months away in the North. She knew that it would appear cowardly not to fight but, as she observes, there is more to life than politics.

Instead, Roy Jenkins stepped into the lists. Jenkins was sometimes caricatured as a man who had never fought for anything in his life except for the best table at a restaurant. That was an unfair and extremely inaccurate view of his character. His decision to fight Warrington was particularly brave. Having been Home Secretary twice, Chancellor of the Exchequer and President of the European Commission, he could easily have ended his political career in humiliating defeat behind the left-wing ex-trade unionist standing for Labour and the London bus-driver standing for the Conservatives.

When Roy Jenkins first set foot in Warrington, he did encounter the odd heckler shouting out 'go back to Brussels, you fat cat'. Asked by journalists about his first impressions of the constituency, he remarked that it had some very fine Victorian architecture. He was never going to appear as a natural man of the people. Increasingly, however, local people came to admire him for taking on such a brave and risky mission. He took to the campaign trail with gusto and determination, and he was remarkably good at engaging with those whom he met. Minders had a real problem dragging him away from conversations in the street so that he kept to his schedule. People liked meeting such a grand figure. They felt, according to one of his key supporters, that they had been blessed. In his memoirs, Roy Jenkins confesses a strong lingering affection for Warrington – soap works, wire factory and all.

The new SDP troops threw themselves into the fight too, and so did the Liberals. The contest did a great deal to strengthen the ties between the two parties. Most of the SDP MPs had held safe Labour seats and many of them were initially disdainful towards the Liberals. At Warrington, they developed much greater respect for their allies' political street-fighting ways.

The proximity of the Liberal local council bastion of Liverpool was a help. Chris Rennard, already the veteran of many campaigns at the age of twenty-two, came over with a group of Liberal activists and was slightly put out to be instructed to undergo the SDP's canvassing training before being let loose on the streets. The SDP's techniques had been lifted straight from the Labour Party. Canvassers were told to mark people simply as for, against or doubtful. Rennard explained that it was helpful to know whether the doubtfuls were soft Tories or soft Labour. The SDP nonetheless resented the impression, which some Liberals gave, that they had no experience of campaigning. Many of them were veterans of large numbers of election campaigns. But their style of campaigning had been different and, at first at least, they had reservations about the Liberal no-holds-barred approach.

There was no serious expectation of winning. Nobody in the campaign regarded this as anything other than a testing of the water. Roy Jenkins set out the issues in a speech explaining how the new politics would tackle the unemployment which was such a large local and national issue. The old politics, he said, were largely to blame. 'The effect of politics in our traditional adversarial, in-and-out, blame-the-other-side-for-everything style, has given our industry one of the least stable frameworks of almost any industrialised country in the world within which to plan and develop the future.'

He went on to attack the 'doctrinaire and incompetent monetarism' of the Thatcherites and the extremism of the Labour Party. He accused the old Labour right of selling the pass: 'Who would have thought a few years ago that first Mr Foot would have become Leader and that then, within six months of his election, he would be being bitterly attacked for being too right-wing a leader?'

Roy Jenkins', performance in the by-election surprised even his admirers. It became clear that, far from finding it an ordeal, he actually enjoyed himself on the stump. As Jo Grimond was later to say of him admiringly, 'This is no fat cat sipping claret instead of cream but a taker of risks and a formidable vote-getter.'

The eventual result was sensational. The polls had steadily predicted a comfortable Labour win, with the vote for the incumbent party around double that for the SDP. The actual result showed the SDP cutting the 10,000 majority to 1,750 with a 42.4% share, against Labour's 48.4%. The Tory Stan Sorrel, who had been referred to as Stan Laurel by the Home Secretary William Whitelaw during the campaign, polled 7.1% and lost his deposit. The Government was indeed in a fine mess.

Roy Jenkins said at the count that the outcome was the first parliamentary election he had ever lost but 'by far the biggest victory in which I have ever participated'. At a press conference the next morning, he was in ebullient mood. When he had first raised the possibility of a new party, he had referred to it as 'an experimental plane'. Asked what stage the experimental plane had now reached, he said that it was at cruising height, passengers were permitted to unfasten their seat-belts and drinks were being served in the first-class section of the cabin. Much of the press agreed. The *Guardian* wrote, 'There have been false dawns before: but there has been no time when a fundamental change in the pattern of British politics looked more likely to come than it does this morning.'

Before the Warrington result was declared, another vacancy had arisen because of the death of the Conservative MP for Croydon North-West. There was a deal between the SDP and the Liberals that they would fight alternate by-elections. So it was the Liberals' turn. The Liberal candidate at the general election had been a local government officer called William Pitt. He had fought the seat three times, with ever diminishing success. In 1979, he had lost his deposit.

With his thin beard and thinner voice, Pitt encapsulated the caricature of the old Liberal Party. He had an illustrious name for a prospective politician, but not a great deal else to recommend him. He did, however, possess a strong streak of stubbornness. After Warrington, David Steel believed that the obvious person to fight the seat was Shirley Williams. Shirley Williams herself, having been accused of ducking the fight in Warrington, was keen to contest as well. But Pitt dug in, and refused to be pushed aside.

The issue was covered in great detail by the media. By the end of the week when it had surfaced, Pitt had made numerous radio and television appearances. After a while, when interviewers suggested to him that he was not as well known as Shirley Williams, he could reply, 'Well, I am now.'

Shirley Williams withdrew gracefully. David Owen, who thought that she could have actually won Warrington, believed that she should have contested the Croydon seat against Pitt, but he did not make this view public.

As the party which had previously held the seat, the Conservatives had the right to choose the date of the by-election, and they did not move the writ until the autumn. The delay until 22 October allowed the Liberals to build up support in the constituency. The Government was in deeper trouble than ever, with unemployment high and splits between wets and dries in the Cabinet dominating the news.

Pitt, who was described as a Liberal–SDP Alliance candidate, won Croydon North-West with a majority of 3,254. His vote share had gone from below 11% to 40%. He managed to inject bathos even into his moment of greatest triumph. As over-enthusiastic supporters starting spraying him with champagne, he turned on them shouting 'Not on my best suit. Not on my wife's best suit.' The quote featured again and again on news programmes. As a sound bite encapsulating the great break-through which the new Alliance had achieved, it left something to be desired. But as the Alliance high command observed, if they could win with Bill Pitt, they could win with anyone.

By this time, the conference season had come and gone. There had been scenes of triumph on both Liberal and SDP platforms. One of the most rousing meetings in twentieth-century political history took place on the fringe of the Liberal assembly in Llandudno. The speakers were Roy Jenkins and Shirley Williams from the SDP and David Steel and Jo Grimond from the Liberals. Grimond's presence was particularly signif-icant, as he had been one of the Liberal MPs least enthusiastic about the new party.

Grimond was given a standing ovation before he uttered a word. In his speech, he urged the new party not to get bogged down in the detail of policy. He went on: 'Make sure that your major policies are right and that you are going to defend them – because you may have to put them into practice.'

When Roy Jenkins spoke, he used a description to which he frequently referred in the months ahead. 'We are united,' he said, 'we can therefore honourably achieve not a marriage of convenience but a partnership of principle.' The audience felt that the mould of British politics really had been broken. Old Liberals were transported back to the heydays of Lloyd George and Asquith. Younger Liberals had been given a vision of the future. There were many moist eyes in the hall.

The next day, the Liberal Party passed a motion calling for an electoral pact with the SDP by 1,600 votes to 112. David Steel in his closing speech delivered the line by which his leadership is best remem-bered: 'I have the good fortune to be the first Liberal Leader for over half a century who is able to say to you at the end of our annual assembly: go back to your constituencies and prepare for government.'

The line was subsequently much mocked and parodied. Playing on Steel's perceived impatience with Liberal grass-roots activists, a sketch in a subsequent Liberal revue had Steel saying, 'Go back to your constituencies and bloody well stay there.' At the time, however, the sentiment did not seem over the top. The Alliance were, after all, still leading in the polls.

Steel did not only tell his troops to prepare for government. He was preparing for government himself by discussing with his MPs what jobs they might have as ministers. Russell Johnston, then Liberal foreign affairs spokesman, remembers being approached by the leader and asked if he would mind David Owen becoming Alliance Foreign Secretary. He told a relieved David Steel that what he really wanted to be was member of the European Commission.

The SDP introduced an innovation for their first conference. It was to be a rolling conference, beginning in Perth, then moving by train to Bradford and ending up in London. By this means, far more supporters could attend one or another part of the conference. Over 5,000 came to one or another of the venues. The train journeys, particularly the leg from Perth to Bradford, became a legend in the party. Only those who had ridden the 'train of shame' could count as true pioneers. The train had to stop at Newcastle to take on fresh supplies.

The rolling conference gave a great impression of dynamism. But the most significant events of the week involved the appearance on the party's platform of five more Labour MPs who had decided to defect to the SDP. Some of them were very significant catches for the new party. Tom McNally was a rising star who had worked for Jim Callaghan in Downing Street and had only entered Parliament in 1979. Dr Dickson Mabon was a former minister. George Cunningham, who was the MP for Islington South and Finsbury, had a reputation as an outstanding parliamentarian.

Rumours flew around about many other potential converts. It was widely and quite falsely believed that the cricketer Geoffrey Boycott was going to be produced on the platform at Bradford. As the year went on, still more Labour MPs rallied to the SDP banner, one or two of them so obscure that they had the journalists busy scanning the pages of the *Times Guide to the House of Commons* to find out if they really were Members of Parliament. All the same, there was a tremendous sense of momentum and exhilaration.

At the Labour conference at the end of September, the SDP came within an ace of receiving an even bigger boost. Tony Benn had challenged Denis Healey for the Deputy Leadership of the party. When the votes were counted, Healey scraped home by the narrowest possible margin, 50.426% to 49.574%. If it had gone the other way, according to Denis Healey's autobiography *The Time of My Life*, 'there would have been a haemorrhage of Labour defections to the SDP both in Parliament and in the country'. The Labour Party could not have recovered. Peter Mandelson, for instance, had many friends at that time in the SDP. They firmly believe that he would have come over if Benn had been elected.

During the Bradford leg of the SDP conference, there had been another significant event. Shirley Williams had announced, without having consulted very many other people, that she intended to fight the newly vacant seat of Crosby. A solid Tory bastion on the edge of Labour Merseyside, Crosby looked like a tough proposition. As Shirley Williams put it, it was a high mountain, but even the highest of mountains had to be scaled.

There were some particular obstacles for Shirley Williams. Although a Roman Catholic, she refused on principle to give the militants of SPUC, the Society for the Protection of the Unborn Child, the totally uncritical support which they demanded. They mounted a vigorous campaign against her as a result. Secondly, the candidate was a former Education Secretary and a great champion of comprehensive schools. With Merchant Taylors' School within the constituency, there were many in Crosby who were zealous supporters of independent education.

Jo Grimond came to campaign in Crosby and made an impassioned speech in favour of private schools. Shirley Williams says that she found this contribution about as helpful as a sock in the jaw.

The Alliance, however, was at the height of its popularity. Shirley Williams's campaign benefited from her huge energy and the great appeal which she had for the electorate. It was difficult to move her down a street at much more than a hundred yards an hour because of all the people who wanted to speak to her. She was, as Richard Holme describes her, 'an incomparable election fighting machine of great stamina and toughness of mind'. The SDP turned out in force. The party's 'Chariots of Fire' theme tune was heard all over the constituency. And the Liberals from nearby Liverpool poured in to help too.

The SDP campaign was helped by the choice of Tory candidate. John Butcher was out of his depth. This was the heyday of the journalistic by-election circus. The parties were expected to stage daily press conferences, a tradition which has now lapsed. In the 1980s, reporters tended to hunt as a pack from one party headquarters to the next and were quick to pounce on a weak or wounded candidate. The doyens of the group were Vincent Hanna of the BBC's *Newsnight* programme and Robert Carvel, the veteran political editor of the *Evening Standard*. With Keith Raffan of the *Daily Express* and Godfrey Barker of the *Daily Telegraph*, they made mincemeat of the unfortunate Mr Butcher.

Carvel's questions were particularly devastating. One day he asked Butcher what it felt like to see a 19,000 majority trickle away through your fingers. Another morning, when the agent arrived late and breathless at the Conservative press conference to announce new canvass returns, Carvel suggested that he might like to come to the front of the room so that reporters could watch his expression while he was feeding them these new lies. Well before polling day, the Conservatives raised a metaphorical white flag over their headquarters, announcing that they would no longer hold daily press conferences.

Shirley Williams scored an enormous triumph. Her majority in this previously 'true blue' seat was 5,289. When the victorious candidate quoted John Dryden 'It is well old age is out and time to begin anew', she could be justified in feeling that the mould of British politics had indeed been broken. A Gallup poll the following month put the Alliance on 51%, compared with 23% for the Conservatives. Translated into seats, it would have given the Alliance nearly 600 out of the 635 in the Commons.

Even the most experienced people in the SDP began to believe that the Alliance was now heading for government. Bill Rodgers says that between Crosby and the Falklands War he thought that the two parties really were in sight of a big breakthrough. In fact, Crosby marked the high-water mark of the Alliance.

One of the reasons that the tide began to recede was the difficulty between the two parties over seat allocation. The SDP became increasingly impatient with the Liberals' insistence on local autonomy, while the Liberals were increasingly suspicious of what they saw as the SDP's lack of understanding of due democratic process.

Bill Rodgers was the SDP's senior national negotiator. By Christmas 1981, the talks were becoming bogged down. Rodgers was particularly impatient with what he regarded as the Liberals' failures to stick to agreements which they had already made. An attempt by the Liberal negotiators to unstitch a deal for Nottinghamshire and Derbyshire provoked him to an unwise move. He told Anthony Howard of the *Observer* about his exasperation with the Liberals and his plan to break off negotiations, and the story became front-page news.

It would be entirely unfair to blame Bill Rodgers for precipitating a slide in the Alliance's fortunes. Much of the press had been viewing the new political phenomenon through rose-tinted spectacles. Like so many objects of press hype, there was bound to come a time when the newspapers would tire of puffing the Alliance up and decide that it was more fun to start deflating it again.

Nevertheless, there was a feeling after the *Observer* story that the new politics were not perhaps quite as new as advertised. Back-room rows over horse-trading sounded awfully like the old politics of the Labour Party. On the scale of grand political showdowns of our time, this was a pretty minor one. But it was the first occasion that an internal dispute within the Alliance had attracted national publicity, and damage was inevitably done.

Following the *Observer* story, I was asked by ITN to go up to a snow-covered Ettrick Bridge to seek the reaction of David Steel. Steel had conferred with Richard Holme by telephone in advance of my visit, and I found him when we arrived at his most disarming and emollient, determined to play the row down. As he explains in his autobiography *Against Goliath*, 'I quickly changed into a woolly sweater on learning that an ITN crew was on its way to Ettrick Bridge, sat in my armchair by a roaring log fire and suggested that Bill must have had too many mince pies for Christmas.'

If there is a lesson for the future in this episode, it is that infighting invariably does great damage to political causes. People feel that if the politicians who are on the same side cannot be loyal to one another, they forfeit their claim on the loyalty of the electors. Hitherto, the Alliance had profited considerably from its apparent unity, compared with the struggles between left and right in the Labour Party and between wets and dries in the Conservatives. The comparison was now not so clear cut.

Soon, however, there was an event which helped to unite the two Alliance parties again. The MP for Glasgow Hillhead Tam Galbraith died, and there was to be another by-election. Hillhead was more promising territory for the Alliance than were the previous seats which had become vacant since its formation. There were Alliance local councillors there, and the constituency had a very helpful profile. It contained Glasgow University, and the SDP had a strong appeal to academic communities. The SDP also drew disproportionate support from professional people and Hillhead was home to no fewer than 1,300 medical doctors.

There was an obvious candidate in Roy Jenkins. When he first heard that Galbraith was dead, Jenkins assumed that the news referred to the distinguished North American economist. Once he found out that it was a death involving a by-election, he was eager to try again to resume his career in Parliament.

Robert Maclennan, who was related to a significant cross-section of the Hillhead electorate, was convinced that this was the ideal seat for his old friend. It remained to persuade the Liberal Party, which already had a candidate in place, to stand down. Russell Johnston conveyed the news back to Maclennan that they were unwilling to do so. Ignoring Jenkins' sinstructions not to put any pressure on the Liberals if they were unwilling to co-operate, Maclennan told Johnston that he would call a press conference to announce that the SDP intended to break off any deal with the Liberals in Scotland unless he heard by eight in the morning that the Liberals were standing down for Roy Jenkins. Just before the deadline, the telephone rang and Jenkins became the candidate. Maclennan never told Jenkins about the strong-arm tactics which had been used to secure the nomination.

Roy Jenkins had the disadvantage of not being Scottish, but this was not held to be a fatal drawback in such a cosmopolitan part of Glasgow. In any case, he was Welsh, which was better to Scottish eyes than being English.

The Alliance was still big news. Among the journalists covering the campaign was a team from CBS in the United States who travelled around in a pink Rolls-Royce. The story was enhanced by the fact that the outcome of the contest was by no means a foregone conclusion. The seat could have gone any one of three ways.

The Tory candidate was Gerry Malone, who left politics in 1997 with the rare distinction of having been defeated in three different constituencies at different times in his career by three different politicians from the third party: David Steel, Roy Jenkins and Mark Oaten. The high point of Malone's campaign was a stunt involving Tory activists spelling the name 'Malone' out in cars in a large car park. A crane was hired to allow TV cameramen to capture this rare piece of performance art for the evening news. Unfortunately the crane did not go quite high enough, and the cameramen could only achieve an image of the word 'alone'.

Labour fielded a left-winger called David Wiseman, known normally to sport an ear-ring, which he removed for the duration of the campaign. My cameraman amused himself during the campaign by trying to shoot close-ups of the hole in the ear which the ring had left.

The Hillhead campaign had a different feel from Warrington. The SDP organised large numbers of coffee mornings for local people to meet the candidate, which suited the genteel ways of the area. There were also enormous public meetings. At the Hyndland School, over a thousand came to hear Roy Jenkins. Old ladies who could not get into the hall itself sat outside in the playground in sub-zero temperatures on school benches, listening to the speeches being relayed on loudspeakers.

By now, the Alliance was in the mid-thirties in the national opinion polls, substantially down from the peak. It was by no means clear that the SDP would win Hillhead. Twelve days before polling day, the *Observer* published an NOP poll which had Roy Jenkins a bad third. For a moment the campaign appeared to have lost its collective nerve.

The setback soon served, however, to galvanise the SDP into greater action. Jenkins would go around on the back of the campaign Land Rover, speaking through a loudhailer and waving to passers-by. At one of his last press conferences, asked how things were going, he replied that he had noticed 'much responsive waving in the nodal areas of the constituency'. On the night, Jenkins won by a respectable margin of 2,000. All four members of the Gang of Four were now back in the House of Commons.

There was a late scare on polling day for the SDP. A maverick candidate had changed his name to Roy Jenkins to try and confuse the voters. The SDP ran up a set of sandwich boards to be paraded outside polling stations with the words 'The Real Roy Jenkins' and his number on the ballot paper. Among those enlisted to wear one of these boards was a Glasgow University student called Charles Kennedy, a leader who can thus almost literally say that his debut on the political stage was as a spear-carrier.

Mrs Thatcher was believed to have a real feeling of apprehension about the return of Roy Jenkins. She feared that he was much more likely to worst her in debate than Labour's Michael Foot. But Jenkins found adjustment to life in the Commons very tough. When he had left in 1976, he had been Home Secretary. He had spent most of his previous Commons career either on the Government or the Opposition front bench. He had difficulty in adapting to third-party status and the lack of a despatch box at which to speak. His strength was a thirty-minute speech full of historical allusions and sophisticated jokes. He found it much harder to make a short sharp impact against a barrage of jeers from the Labour left who, to make matters worse, sat in the same part of the chamber as the SDP.

Subsequent leaders of the Alliance parties and of the Liberal Democrats have had similar problems. They have been most acute when the third party has posed the greatest threat to either or both of the others. During the build-up to the Iraq crisis of 2003, Charles Kennedy was subjected to much the same attack from the Conservatives as Roy Jenkins used to suffer from Labour. No leader of the Liberal Democrats or its predecessor parties has enjoyed the Commons Chamber. Their personal experience of the bear-garden atmosphere has reinforced their political objections to adversarial politics and made them even more passionate in their enthusiasm for change. There was an irony, nonetheless, about Roy Jenkins's re-entry into politics. The expectation had been that he would be a hopeless campaigner but magisterial in the

Commons. In fact, he proved to be highly effective on the stump but disappointing in the House.

The Falklands War began only eight days after Hillhead. It was not at all clear at first that it would restore the fortunes of the Conservative Party. The reverse could easily have been true. The islands had been occupied, apparently, because of the negligence and misjudgement of Conservative ministers. The conflict could even have meant the end of Margaret Thatcher's political career. Indeed, the electorate did not at first seem to be giving her their support. On the first Thursday after the invasion, the Alliance gained a local government seat from the Conservatives.

Nonetheless, the Government soon began to play the patriotism card and to win support with it. As the conflict wore on, Margaret Thatcher was able to portray herself as a courageous war leader. Apart from the Argentine forces, the Alliance were the biggest losers of the Falklands War. The effect was noticed almost immediately at the SDP's Cowley Street headquarters. Membership applications had been running at four hundred a week before the invasion of the islands. Thereafter they precipitously dropped to two hundred.

Had the Beaconsfield by-election been held before the outbreak of hostilities, it would have marked the fourth gain of the Parliament for the Alliance. The Liberal candidate, Paul Tyler, was an ex-MP and an experienced and skilled campaigner. Labour's man, on the other hand, a young unknown barrister then known as Anthony rather than Tony Blair, was standing for a party with an extremist programme which went down like a lead balloon in well-heeled Buckinghamshire. His election address called for withdrawal from the EEC and from NATO; on the stump he preferred to concentrate on the local issue of gravel pits.

The Conservatives had a much stronger issue, support for 'our boys'. They put out a leaflet which included a photograph of the Tory agent, who happened to be a reservist, in full battle-dress. This featured considerably more prominently than the picture of the candidate Tim Smith.

Smith duly won the seat and remained the MP until he had to stand down in 1997 for taking money from Mohammed Al Fayed. Paul Tyler had the consolation of not having to swap his house in Cornwall for the much smaller one which would have been all he could have afforded at Buckinghamshire prices. He had the further satisfaction of beating Anthony Blair into third place and seeing him lose his deposit.

By-elections had been the oxygen of the SDP–Liberal Alliance's rise. This was the first serious electoral setback which the new political force had suffered. From the vantage-point of 2003, it is striking how many by-elections there were between Warrington in July 1981 and Beaconsfield in May 1982. These days, MPs tend to be younger and fitter, and very few incumbents leave Parliament, like Sir Tom Williams in Warrington, to take up other occupations. It means that it is harder for a third party to attract the excitement and publicity which a by-election brings.

The Falklands were not the only cause of the Thatcher Government's revival. Inflation had begun to fall, and the rise in unemployment was levelling off. Meanwhile, real incomes of those in work were rising significantly. Much of the Alliance's support had come from dissatisfied former Conservatives. Now they began to return to their former allegiance.

Another result of the Falklands War was that the spotlight within the Alliance fell very much on David Owen. He had been Foreign Secretary, and his contributions to the debates on the Falklands commanded considerable respect. He was broadly supportive of the Thatcher Government's stance, and as the MP for the Plymouth dockyards, sounded both knowledgeable and patriotic. He also, however, made some telling criticisms, both about the miscalculations which had led to the invasion and about the plans for the aftermath, which he believed should include a role for the United Nations. This was to stand Owen in good stead when the new party came to elect its first Leader. Hitherto, it had functioned under the collective command of the Gang of Four. Now the members were asked to elect a single Leader. Journalists found the MPs who had presented such a solid front in their breakaway from the Labour Party now campaigning hard against each other in the rival camps.

Originally, Shirley Williams had looked a likely contender for the Leadership, but she decided instead to stand for the position of President of the Party, and gave her support to David Owen's campaign for Leader. Roy Jenkins, meanwhile, had the backing of Bill Rodgers. Because of Owen's performance on the Falklands, the result was much closer than it would have been before. An NOP poll for the *Observer* showed a large lead for Owen over Jenkins amongst all voters. It was of course, however, only the members of the SDP who were eligible to decide. When their votes were counted, Roy Jenkins won with 26,300 to Owen's 20,900.

On the surface, the contest was amicable enough, but it did become clear to outsiders for the first time that there were two distinct factions within the SDP. The key division between them was over their attitude to the Liberals, with the Jenkinsites much better disposed to their allies and the Owenites far more suspicious. Ideological differences were much less clear. At one time, David Owen had been much more attached to the idea of the SDP being a party of the left, while Roy Jenkins was regarded as a centrist. Soon Owen was being depicted as clearly to the right of Jenkins.

After Beaconsfield, the Alliance suffered another reverse. Bruce Douglas-Mann, the MP for Mitcham and Morden, had been one of the last Labour members to switch to the SDP. Unlike all the previous defectors, he decided that the honourable course of action was to resign his seat and fight a by-election under his new colours. This decision was not greatly welcomed by the other members of the SDP parliamentary party. They had held to the convention that an MP is elected as an individual to represent his/her constituents, not as a spokesman for a political party. In any case, they claimed, they remained true to the beliefs on which they had originally been elected; it was their old party which had changed its views. Neville Sandelson memorably berated Douglas-Mann on this point as they toured the constituency on a loud-speaking tour during the by-election. Sandelson would alternately switch the loud-speaker on to sing Douglas-Mann's praises to the electorate and switch it off to curse the candidate to his face for his stupidity. Douglas-Mann duly lost the seat. Subsequent defectors to the Liberal Democrats reverted to the old constitutional convention, but the counter-example of Bruce Douglas-Mann was always on hand for opponents to cite.

Morale in both the SDP and the Liberal Party inevitably suffered as 1982 went on. David Steel did his best to rally the Liberals at their autumn Assembly in Bournemouth. He accused Mrs Thatcher of 'wrapping herself in the Falklands bunting'. She should learn, he said, 'that there is a difference between patriotism and jingoism'. This time, he did not repeat his injunction to go back and prepare for government, preferring the rather less ambitious-sounding phrase 'we are ready to govern' for his peroration.

The SDP decided to repeat their rolling-conference experiment. The second year inevitably lacked the élan which the first had engendered. Following sessions in Cardiff and Derby, the third leg of the conference was scheduled for Great Yarmouth. The train taking the delegates broke down in the fens some distance short of the destination. A railway official announced to the despondent passengers, 'There'll be another engine in March.' It came as some relief for them to discover that March was the name of a place in East Anglia as well as of a month.

The Great Yarmouth leg of the conference was the first session where the delegates had been democratically selected. They were therefore able to vote on policy; previous sessions had only held consultative debates. The deadline for amendments was the eve of the Conference. The National Organiser Dick Newby got off the train in the early hours and had to spend the whole of the night sorting out the agenda. After that the rolling-conference idea was shelved. The balance between exciting innovation and logistical nightmare had shifted decisively.

The issue of the Alliance leadership still remained unresolved. Eventually it was decided that Roy Jenkins would be the Alliance choice for Prime Minister if the two parties were to form a Government, while David Steel was to be the leader of the campaign. The press took up the cumbersome title of 'Prime Minister Designate' for Jenkins, a label which nobody in either party liked much. There were doubts in many quarters about the wisdom of the arrangement. Steel was measured to be much more popular than Jenkins by the opinion polls. On the other hand, Roy Jenkins had been Chancellor and Home Secretary, while David Steel had never held office. A messy situation was saved by the genuine regard which Steel and Jenkins had for each other.

Before the end of the Parliament, there were two further by-elections of great significance to the Alliance. The first was in Bermondsey, where Labour had selected a gift standard-bearer for the Alliance, a far-left crusading gay-rights activist called Peter Tatchell. Tatchell had been denounced by the Labour Leader Michael Foot, but still remained the candidate. A former Southwark Council Leader, John O'Grady, stood as Independent Labour, and was an early favourite. But the press had underestimated the young barrister fighting for the Liberals, Simon Hughes.

So far during the Parliament, each Alliance success had been at the expense of the Conservatives: Croydon North-West, Crosby and Hillhead had all had Tory MPs before they were won. Now the Tories had revived, but Labour remained highly vulnerable. Bermondsey had always been rock-solid working-class Labour. When the SDP was first formed, it had been assumed that it would stand more chance in Labour seats while the Liberals would do better against the Conservatives. The evidence, however, was that both parties appealed to the same kind of voter. It is unlikely that any SDP candidate would have performed better in the Bermondsey by-election than Simon Hughes, who had campaigned assiduously on the ground for the past two years.

When Hughes joined the Liberal Party in Bermondsey, he increased the local membership from six to seven people. By the time he fought the GLC election in 1981, he was able to increase the vote from 2.3% to 15%. Then in 1982, the party won 25% of the vote in the local elections. This was a predictable by-election; the Labour MP Robert Mellish had left the Labour Party and had been threatening to precipitate a contest for some time. By the time the independent Labour candidate O'Grady announced that he was in the race, the Liberals had put in three months' solid work. The decisive factor was an opinion poll putting the Liberals in second place on 27%, ahead of O'Grady's 24%. Tatchell still scored 42%, but Simon Hughes was able to argue that he was the only candidate who could beat him. In the end, he won with a majority of over 9,000 and 58% of the vote. Still more remarkably, he has contested the seat successfully at the five subsequent general elections.

The bandwagon was rolling again. A further vacancy arose when the Labour MP for Darlington died. Early polling in the seat showed that the Alliance was ahead. Here, it was the SDP's turn to fight, and their candidate was a local TV journalist, Tony Cook.

Poor Mr Cook suffered the same fate as the Conservative candidate in Crosby. The by-election media circus turned up, as usual, sniffing for blood, and Tony Cook quickly emerged as the most vulnerable, the least experienced and the least knowledgeable of the candidates. He may have been good at asking questions, but he had great trouble answering them. Emergency training sessions for him at the SDP's Cowley Street headquarters had little effect. He floundered his way through a campaign in which his opinion poll lead rapidly disappeared. He was sunk, above all, by his performance in a *Newsnight* debate between the candidates, chaired by that nemesis of so many weak contenders, Vincent Hanna. Cook came in a poor third, behind both Labour and the Conservatives.

In an internal memo analysing the reasons for the failure, Bill Rodgers wrote that Cook should not be regarded as a scapegoat: 'He is a decent man and deserves the greatest credit for surviving the immense personal battering he received.' But the memo goes on: 'He had very little knowledge of politics and showed limited aptitude for learning … It is difficult to escape the conclusion that he was almost the worst candidate we could have chosen to fight a crucial by-election under close scrutiny and in a town which took its politics seriously.'

Darlington stopped the Alliance recovery in its tracks. Had the SDP won, the victory would have represented an invaluable launch-pad for the 1983 general election. On the other hand, if Labour had lost, they might well have ditched their Leader. Without Michael Foot, Labour could have done considerably better in the general election. The 'what if?' question is not a simple one to answer. Nor is it fair to blame the hapless Tony Cook entirely for the debacle. The system that selected him had its flaws too. And that in turn was the product of the fact that the SDP was still a very new party which was feeling its way.

Meanwhile, the interminable seat allocation struggle between the two Alliance parties was at last coming to an end. There remained only three constituencies where agreement was impossible, and the two parties ended up fighting each other. The most serious consequences were suffered in the potentially winnable Liverpool Broadgreen. The SDP claimed the seat for Richard Crawshaw, the sitting member for a seat at the other side of the city which had been carved up under the boundary reorganisation. The Liberals held eleven of the fifteen council seats in Broadgreen, and strongly resisted ceding their hard-won territory to the SDP. A deal was almost agreed involving Crawshaw ceding his claim along with the Liberal Simon Knott in Hammersmith and another Liberal, Jeff Roberts, in Hackney. In the end, Roberts refused to budge.

Crawshaw then followed suit and the Militant Terry Fields won Broadgreen, with the Liberal Richard Pine third and Crawshaw fourth.

On the whole, however, the seat negotiations produced results with which both parties could live. Some have suggested that, given the eventual outcome of the 1983 election, with seventeen victorious Liberals and only six Social Democrats, the SDP had made a poor bargain. In fact, had the two parties won a hundred seats, as they hoped they would, instead of twenty-three, the distribution between them would have been almost exactly equal.

Compared with the enormous expectations of late 1981 and early 1982, the Alliance went into the 1983 election in a somewhat weakened state. By May, they were registering a bare 14% in the polls. The election that followed, however, was to follow the pattern of February 1974, with the prospect of breakthrough becoming a real possibility, but only late in the campaign.

As always, success or failure for the Alliance depended as much on the behaviour of the other parties as on their own performance. It was clear that the Labour Party was very vulnerable in 1983. The manifesto was memorably described by Gerald Kaufman as the 'longest suicide note in history'. Labour were committed to renationalisation, unilateral disarmament, import controls and leaving the Common Market. The sentence in the manifesto on this last issue amply justifies the Kaufman description: 'The next Labour Government, committed to radical, socialist policies for reviving the British economy, is bound to find continued membership a most serious obstacle to the fulfilment of those policies.' This was the manifesto on which the former Labour candidate for Beaconsfield, Anthony Blair, now standing in Sedgefield, first entered Parliament.

The Alliance manifesto was entitled 'Working Together for Britain'. It called for an end to confrontation politics. Many of the measures, like prices and incomes policy, an emphasis on training, partnership in industry, decentralisation, electoral reform and community policing, were familiar from previous Liberal manifestos. The distinction from previous elections lay in the fact that 1983 saw the widest gap between Labour and the Conservatives of any campaign in post-war history. It left an obvious space for the Alliance.

The manifesto resonated with attacks on the extremism of the other two parties. Thus the passage on defence reads, 'Our defence policies reject both Labour's one-sided disarmament and the Conservatives' escalation of the nuclear arms race.' On industrial policy, it says, 'The policies offered by the two class-based parties will further divide the nation North v South, Management v Labour.' On unemployment, it observes, 'Mrs Thatcher's government stands idly by, hoping that the blind forces of the marketplace will restore the jobs and factories that its indifference has destroyed. The Labour Party's response is massive further nationalisation, a centralised state socialist economy and rigid controls over enterprise.' In the circumstances of 1983, the tactic of even-handedness, of being equally critical of Labour and the Conservatives, made every sense.

The Alliance's approach was sometimes described as 'a better yesterday'. The parties were criticised for harking back to failed corporatist policies of the 1960s. But there was much in the manifesto which had never been tried, notably the proposals for devolution and electoral reform. Twenty years on, Charles Kennedy can say with pride that he stands by the platform on which he fought his first general election. Tony Blair could certainly not say the same.

In some ways, the two parties were surprisingly unprepared for the 1983 election campaign. Hitherto, they had functioned completely separately, with the SDP at 4 Cowley Street and the Liberals in part of the National Liberal Club. Even the MPs had only held four joint meetings of the two parliamentary parties. Now it was decided that the combined staff of both parties, together with those drafted in especially for the campaign, would all crowd together into the rabbit warren of offices in Cowley Street.

There was not even a joint SDP–Liberal campaign committee in existence. One was hastily cobbled together, but it was only to meet at weekends, since most of its members were on the campaign trail. A handful of peers, together with a few experienced hands like Paul Tyler, were to hold the fort in between times. Lord Diamond, a former Treasury Minister and close SDP ally of Roy Jenkins, presided over the makeshift arrangements at Cowley Street, where at the outset the newly installed telephone system failed to work.

One of the problems which beset the Alliance in the early weeks of the campaign was the dual leadership. TV would cover David Steel and Roy Jenkins on alternate days, but Jenkins had a very marginal seat to defend, so was not travelling nearly as much as Steel. The Jenkins footage would often not look as good as the Steel coverage.

There was one day in particular when the BBC had decided that its focus was to be Roy Jenkins. The SDP Leader had decided to go to Ayr to repay a debt. The candidate there was Chic Brodie, the Liberal who had displayed much graciousness in the manner in which he had stepped aside in Hillhead for the by-election. But the seat was a poor prospect for the Alliance; there were few troops on the ground and Roy Jenkins was seen staging a less than inspiring walkabout in the rain. The same day, David Steel addressed 2,000 supporters in sunshine in Hereford, not a frame of which made the television bulletins.

The one special role which Jenkins had been assigned as a result of his Prime Minister Designate status was to be the Alliance interviewee on the two big set-piece TV programmes of the election, *Panorama* and *Weekend World*. His performance was judged defensive and ponderous. A Harris poll asked which of the two Alliance leaders would make the best Prime Minister. The answer was embarrassing to Jenkins; it was 65% for Steel and 22% for Jenkins. The Liberals became more and more restive.

In a move which, after the election, was to lead to David Steel to call for his resignation, Tony Greaves of the Association of Liberal Councillors had already circulated to Liberal candidates a line-by-line briefing on the differences between the manifesto and Liberal policy, designed to demonstrate how the SDP had watered it down. The Young Liberals even less helpfully had put out a press statement saying the manifesto was not worth voting for. Now, however, discontent was spreading to more mainstream activists, who deluged headquarters with demands for changes at the top.

Several senior Liberals came to the conclusion that Roy Jenkins should be deposed from his role as Prime Minister Designate and that David Steel should be acknowledged as the one leader of the Alliance campaign. Steel himself reluctantly agreed to the strategy. The coup was to be staged at a weekend 'summit' at his house in Ettrick Bridge. This occasion had originally been conceived as a media stunt to attract publicity to the Alliance at the same time as the Prime Minister was at the Williamsburg Summit in the USA with President Reagan. Now it was to assume genuine political significance.

David Steel had sounded out Roy Jenkins before the meeting. He had been very negative about the idea. Then at the summit itself, Steel produced a draft press release announcing the change. John Pardoe and the other Liberals present spoke strongly in favour of it. Most of the main SDP participants took the opposite line equally vociferously. Shirley Williams, Bill Rodgers and Jack Diamond regarded Steel's actions as underhand and treacherous. The Liberals knew that the plan would only work with Jenkins's consent. When it was clear that this was not forthcoming, they dropped it.

The occasion provoked considerable bad blood between the SDP and the Liberals. The weather was partly to blame. Fog delayed the arrival of many of the participants, so that the opportunity for discussion was cut short, and the demand for a change in strategy came much more abruptly. To this day, the SDP participants claim that they were bounced, while the Liberals say that leading Social Democrats had been forewarned and had agreed to the change over the leadership, but ducked out when it came to the crunch.

There were undoubtedly misunderstandings. Bill Rodgers confirms that he had indeed had a call from David Steel ahead of the meeting, from which he gained the impression that Roy Jenkins had at least not turned down the plan for a change. He later had a call from Jennifer Jenkins, making it quite clear that her husband was in fact firmly opposed to the Liberal plan. It therefore did indeed come as a shock to him when he heard it outlined at the meeting itself. The amazing aspect was that, despite the large numbers of press gathered outside, news of the plot never leaked. The most outsiders could detect was a subtle change in the chemistry between the leading figures of the two parties.

Both Steel and Jenkins subsequently denied, with great plausibility, that personal ambition had dictated the positions which they took at Ettrick Bridge. Steel was genuinely persuaded that the Alliance would do better if he were unambiguously identified as the Leader. He had the polling evidence to prove it. Equally, Jenkins thought that it was highly dangerous to change horses in mid-stream. It would send out a confused signal about the Alliance and could only do it damage. It is impossible to tell which of them was right. Had Steel been clearly identified as the Leader at the beginning of the campaign, the result may well have been better. But the Ettrick Bridge strategy of the Liberals would have carried considerable risk.

In the event, the campaign did gather some momentum after the summit. Roy Jenkins's performances were considered much sharper, and at last the polls began to move. Furthermore, Labour's campaign was lurching from bad to worse. Denis Healey and James Callaghan both voiced their objections to their party's policy for unilateral disarmament. Healey then accused Margaret Thatcher of 'glorying in slaughter' after the Falklands. When a heckler shouted at Neil Kinnock that the Prime Minister had guts, he retorted that it was a pity that British soldiers had had to leave their guts on Goose Green to prove it.

The Conservatives started to worry about the threat from the Alliance. Having largely ignored the Liberal–SDP campaign, they discussed launching an attack against it. An advertisement was prepared with a blank sheet representing Alliance policy. In the end, however, they thought better of this strategy. They may have concluded that anything that drew further attention to their challenge would only benefit the Alliance. This is the calculation which the Conservative and Labour parties have repeatedly made at subsequent elections. Attacking the third party only results in giving it greater salience and credibility.

During the last week of the 1983 campaign, there was a real prospect that the Alliance could overtake the Labour Party. On the final Sunday, a Harris poll for the *Observer* put the Alliance one point ahead of Labour. The actual result fell just short of that figure. The Alliance had 25.4%, the highest percentage share for a third party since 1923. Labour ended up with 27.6%, just over two points better. It was a very close-run thing, but it was a blow to have missed second place so narrowly.

The outcome in seats was a much greater disappointment. The Liberals emerged with seventeen and the SDP with six. Under PR the Alliance would have had not twenty-three seats, but some 160. Twenty-three sitting SDP members were among the losers, including Shirley Williams and Bill Rodgers. Williams was out by just under 3,500, caused largely by a change in her constituency boundaries. Tactically, the SDP made a mistake in not throwing more national party resources into keeping such a key figure in Parliament. Some other SDP members lost by tiny margins, like the 363 votes by which George Cunningham fell short in Islington South, but the majority of SDP MPs came third or even fourth.

The SDP gained only one new MP, Charles Kennedy in Ross, Cromarty and Skye. Kennedy had come over from Indiana, where he was a Fulbright Scholar, the previous year, to be interviewed for a place on the SDP candidates' list. The time allotted for the interview was ten minutes, but the panel were so struck by the flair and maturity of this twenty-two-year-old that they found themselves talking to him for well over double the time he was supposed to have.

Robert Maclennan, who had been the leading interviewer, was also in charge of the seat negotiations in Scotland with the Liberal Party. He was determined to secure the Ross, Cromarty and Skye seat for Kennedy. The Liberals claimed the seat on the grounds that it had actually had a Liberal MP as recently as 1970. Maclennan pointed out that they had come fourth in 1979. Having offered the Liberals Strathkelvin and Bearsden by way of compensation, he paved the way for Kennedy to become the youngest member of the House of Commons.

The Liberals lost only Bill Pitt, and gained five new seats. There were many losing candidates, nonetheless, who had believed that this was the election at which their efforts over the years would be finally rewarded. Alan Watson just missed in Richmond and Barnes by seventy-four and Stuart Mole lost Chelmsford by 378.

A number of explanations have been advanced for the Alliance's relative failure. Some cite the problems over the joint Leadership and the difficulties over Roy Jenkins's role as Prime Minister Designate. The tensions over seat allocation had certainly set the parties back as the Parliament drew to a close. Others note the fact that Alliance supporters identified much less strongly with their parties' policies than Conservative and Labour voters. This helped to make their adherence softer. In some ways, indeed, Alliance policy was not very well defined. SDP MPs had at one point divided three different ways over trade union legislation.

The overwhelming reason, however, was clearly the Falklands War. The charge of extremism against the Labour Party still stuck. But the charge of extremism against the Conservatives had far less resonance by the end of the Parliament. Mrs Thatcher's Government benefited from the perception that they had been responsible for a bold and triumphant military success. There was a phenomenon on the doorsteps known as the 'you've got to hand it to Maggie' syndrome. People did not warm to the Prime Minister, but they felt that she had courage.

This explanation of the 1983 vote gave the Alliance parties some comfort. Despite this special factor, they had made a great advance. Next time, as memories of the war in the Falklands receded, many believed that they really could make the big breakthrough.

6   From Glory Days to Salad Days, 1983–8

If they had been animals, most of the Liberals would have been herbivores, peacefully snuffling around the political undergrowth of community politics or craning their necks to browse on the foliage of high principle and idealism. In 1983, they found themselves yoked to a thoroughgoing carnivore. David Owen came as a shock to the Liberal Party. They had never encountered anything like him.

To this day, Owen is regarded considerably less favourably than the Antichrist in Liberal Democrat circles. The mildest and most reasonable of Liberal Democrats will say that they hate Owen with a passion. The sentiment is felt equally strongly by many of those who worked closely with him in the SDP. There are many from both sides of the Alliance who hold him responsible for destroying the best ever prospect of breakthrough at the 1987 election and then for all but wrecking both the Alliance parties.

There is truth in both charges. It is a little too easy, however, to blame Owen for everything which went wrong. It is important, too, not to overlook his considerable talents. Owen could be a highly effective politician. He had, after all, been Britain's youngest Foreign Secretary since Anthony Eden. He had a strong grasp of policy on a wide variety of subjects, particularly defence. He was to follow up his effective performances in the Falklands War with pronouncements on a wide variety of domestic and foreign issues which attracted attention and support. He started work at dawn and kept up with the news on the wire services hour by hour to make sure that he had a quotable reaction ready before his political opponents. He had the rare advantage for a British politician of good looks and physical presence.

Owen could also be effective in the Commons. He led a party of six, but created the illusion that there were massed ranks behind him. Unlike his predecessor, he positively relished taking on Dennis Skinner and the other Labour left-wingers who competed with the SDP for the front bench below the gangway. Once on the ITN *5.45 News* I described Owen and the Tribunites as 'grown men jostling for seats'. Owen, who was usually more polite to journalists than he was to his colleagues, was furious with me. His argument in essence was one familiar to any schoolteacher: it wasn't me, sir. I was duly rebuked by the Editor for 'editorialising'.

Those whom Owen had crossed liked to relate the mythical story of his christening. The first fairy godmother gave him the gift of good looks. The second one bestowed the blessing of a fine intellect. Then, just as the ceremony was about to end, there was a puff of smoke and the bad fairy burst in to declare, 'My gift to the child is the quality of being a complete shit.'

Back in the realms of reality, many Liberals never really understood that Owen's vision of the SDP was so distinct from that of Roy Jenkins. He believed that the Alliance was necessary for tactical reasons but he thought that the values of the SDP and the Liberals were fundamentally different. He professed bewilderment that people who had just set up a new party should want almost at once to merge it with another one. He looked forward to a time when proportional representation would be introduced so that the parties could compete against each other.

Just as Owen could attract antagonism of unfathomable depth both within the ranks of the SDP and from the Liberal Party, he was capable of commanding deep loyalty as well. Some of the most staunch Owenites like Mike Thomas had been defeated at the 1983 election. But John Cartwright, the MP for Woolwich, had survived. Liked and greatly respected across the entire Alliance, he became Owen's Chief Whip and chief lieutenant. Other dedicated Owenites included the journalist Polly Toynbee, Danny Finkelstein, who had risen up the ranks of the Young Social Democrats and the former Communist, former leader of the National Union of Students Sue Slipman. For all his prickliness towards political colleagues, Owen also had a very good relationship with his own staff.

Owen's succession to the SDP Leadership took the form of a bloodless coup. He declared his intention of standing against Roy Jenkins, but Jenkins had decided to relinquish the Leadership in any case. Owen only hastened the timing. Since the other two members of the Gang of Four had lost their seats, the party did not really have any other choice, and he was elected unopposed.

Up until now, even after Roy Jenkins's election, many of the aspects of the collective leadership of the Gang of Four had persisted. They had met as a mini-Cabinet of the SDP once a week at the restaurant L'Amico in Horseferry Road. Once David Owen took the helm, this tradition ceased. Influence passed instead to a praetorian guard of Owenite loyalists, who were determined to resist any drift towards merger with the Liberals.

David Steel was already looking towards that outcome. It would certainly have saved a great many of the problems which the Alliance suffered in the 1983 election, and avoided the much greater ones which they were to face in 1987. However, Steel recognised that David Owen was a dedicated opponent of merger, and that so long as he could not be moved from that position, the change was not worth considering. In any case, even Social Democrats like Bill Rodgers who were well disposed towards the Liberals believed that merger should not be precipitated; it would work better as an organic process.

Steel himself seriously contemplated resignation. He had led his party for seven years, a feat which had often involved pulling it up by its own boot-straps. The activists were frequently difficult. So too were the MPs, particularly in the immediate wake of the 1983 result, when some felt that he had bungled the Ettrick Bridge coup. Ultimately, he agreed to the compromise of a three-month sabbatical, during which the Chief Whip Alan Beith would hold the fort as acting leader. In these inauspicious circumstances, the era of the two Davids began.

One of the reasons that David Steel's relationship with Roy Jenkins had worked was the difference in their ages. They belonged to different generations and they complemented each other: Jenkins brought the wisdom of an elder statesman to the relationship; Steel brought the vigour of relative youth. Steel and Owen were almost exactly the same age. Even if there had not been clear political differences between them, something akin to sibling rivalry would have been very likely.

David Steel once said that his relationship with David Owen was rather like the marriage between Dame Sybil Thorndike and Lewis Casson. Asked if she had ever contemplated divorce, Dame Sybil said, 'Divorce never, murder frequently.' Steel's friends admired his extraordinary equability in dealing with Owen. At meetings, they say, Owen would slump scowling at the Liberals, not attempting to disguise what he thought of them. David Steel himself remains diplomatic in his language about David Owen. He points out simply that he realised that Owen always had his own agenda. From the early days of the SDP, Steel saw Owen as the mirror image of Cyril Smith. Just as Smith wanted to strangle the SDP at birth, so Owen wanted right from the start to elbow the Liberals aside.

The satirical programme *Spitting Image* developed caricature puppets of the two Davids. David Owen's puppet was far larger than David Steel's. The Steel figure would habitually sit in the Owen figure's pocket. The notion of Steel being completely dominated by Owen was a joke which did real damage, compounded by the fact that some Liberal activists believed that the caricature was accurate.

At the outset, both Davids tried hard to get their relationship off on a friendly basis. Shortly after the 1983 election, they had an amicable meeting at David Owen's country home in Wiltshire. They agreed a formula which was to stick in public for the duration of the Parliament. David Steel would not call for an early merger so long as David Owen did not rule out merger for ever. As a result, the outside world took a long time to become fully aware of the breadth of the gap between the two leaders on the issue.

David Steel duly appeared, refreshed after his sabbatical, to address his party assembly in Harrogate. He did his best to persuade the Liberals that the general election had not been a disappointment but a near triumph. The language of breakthrough was back on the agenda:

> *Of course we still have a long way to go before we reach power –*
> *the power to implement Liberal policies, but another leap*
> *forward at the next election, of the same size as the last one, will*
> *see us there. It has been said that the weakness of our Alliance is*
> *that our vote was evenly spread; that we piled up 313 second*
> *places throughout the land but that our vote was insufficiently*
> *concentrated in specific areas. That may be a short-term*
> *weakness but I believe it to be our long-term strength. We do*
> *appeal to all ages and classes and regions.*

For all Steel's optimism, the continuing existence of two parties instead of one did represent a drain on energy and resources. There were two headquarters with two sets of staff, often duplicating each others' efforts. The phone calls between Cowley Street and the National Liberal Club alone ate into money which would have been better spent on campaigns. Policy-making became a tortuous affair, with separate long debates within each party followed by a further long debate between them.

The Alliance had been held back greatly in the previous Parliament by the issue of seat negotiations. Now the issue was reopened all over again. Many local parties were keen to have joint selections, allowing members of both halves of the Alliance to have a say in the choice of candidate. There were two variations. A closed joint selection meant that the candidate had to belong to the party which had been allocated the seat, but that both Liberal and SDP members could vote. An open joint selection meant that both Liberals and Social Democrats could apply to be the candidate.

David Owen was instinctively opposed to any form of joint selection, open or closed. He was afraid that, since Liberal members outnumbered Social Democrats in the country, the SDP would lose out. Many grass-roots social democrats had formed close working relationships with their counterparts in the Liberal Party, and felt frustrated by the veto from on high. Eventually Bill Rodgers was brought in to sort out the remaining problems from the SDP side. In 1985, he proposed a package to Owen which involved twenty further joint open selections and Owen accepted it.

By this time, David Owen had established complete dominance of the SDP. Politically, he was edging the party to the right. He described his approach as 'tough and tender'. The tough part was his firm commitment to nuclear weapons, a hard line against the union militancy which was to come to the fore during the miners' strike, and support for the market economy. The tender side involved a strong commitment to helping the vulnerable and to ensuring equal educational opportunities and health care for all. Owen was often characterised as being sub-Thatcherite, but at this stage, at least, he was clearly not a Tory.

Nonetheless, Owen's political philosophy meant that the gap was widening with the Liberal Party, particularly on defence. The 1984 Liberal Assembly passed a resolution backed by the new MP for Yeovil Paddy Ashdown which called for the removal of cruise missiles from British soil. Ashdown was not a unilateralist or a member of CND, but he believed that cruise missiles should not be stationed in Britain until this could happen in a context which did not disrupt the multilateral disarmament process. David Steel himself spoke against this resolution, but he was defeated. Defence was to become an ever-growing source of tension as the Parliament went on.

As in the previous Parliament, by-elections were to become very important to the Alliance. There was an early contest in 1983 in Penrith and the Border, caused by the decision to elevate Willie Whitelaw to the House of Lords. The Liberal candidate Michael Young reduced a majority of over 15,000 to 500. The following year, Alliance candidates performed creditably in Stafford and in South-West Surrey. Then, on the same day as the European elections, there was a by-election in Portsmouth South, considered to be a safe Conservative seat.

The Alliance candidate Mike Hancock was a member of the SDP, but he had many of the characteristics of successful Liberal contenders. He was a long-serving member of both Portsmouth City Council and Hampshire County Council and he had fought the 1983 general election against the late and deeply obscure Tory member Bonner Pink. He could campaign as 'Mr Portsmouth'. The Conservative standard-bearer Patrick Rock had the disadvantage of being an outsider, which the Alliance did everything to exploit. Rock compounded the problem at his eve-of-the-poll rally, filmed for ITN, by forgetting in which constituency the main city hospital was located. To add to his difficulties, he had poor back-up from a near-moribund local Conservative Association.

The SDP by-election machine, masterminded by Alec McGivan, had become well oiled and extremely effective. The Liberals claimed that this was because it was now modelled closely on their ideas. Peter Chegwyn, one of the main architects of the Croydon North-West victory three years before, was a Liberal councillor nearby and devised many of the Portsmouth leaflets. SDP and Liberal supporters flooded into the constituency. However, the outcome was far from certain. An NOP poll put the SDP third. Chegwyn seized on a rival survey in the *Birmingham Mail* which put Hancock ahead. His last-minute leaflet, drawing voters' attention to this, neglected to point out that the survey consisted of a completely unscientific sample of around twelve Portsmouth people whom the Political Editor John Lewis happened to have met. Nonetheless, momentum is all-important in a by-election. The leaflet helped to create it and Hancock emerged the victor with a majority of 1,341 – the first SDP candidate outside the Gang of Four to win a by-election.

The Euro-elections the same day were a disappointment, not so much in terms of the 19.5% percentage share, but because the Alliance failed to win a single seat. The size of the Euro-constituencies magnified the distortions caused by the 'first past the post' system and made the contests even less fair than Westminster elections.

There were two further by-election victories in the Parliament which were Liberal triumphs. First Richard Livsey captured Brecon and Radnor. Livsey was a salt-of-the-earth local farmer who went on to serve his constituents with diligence and to be a greatly respected leader of the Welsh Liberal Democrats. The campaign fought on his behalf was rather less respectable. The description of Livsey's 'secure family background' was deliberately aimed at the less orthodox domestic arrangements of his opponents.

Then Elizabeth Shields won the apparently safe Tory seat of Ryedale, overturning a majority of more than 15,000. The same day, the Liberal

Chris Walmsley missed winning the equally safe Tory seat of West Derbyshire by a mere hundred votes. The Liberals lacked the financial resources of the SDP, and their organisation was stretched to the limits by having to fight two contests at once. The Tories may well have saved themselves in West Derbyshire by putting out some effective disinformation exaggerating the chances of the Labour Party. This rearguard action to stop Labour supporters voting tactically was mainly the work of the former MP, Matthew Parris, who had caused the by-election by standing down to become a TV presenter. He admits in his autobiography that he was acting to assuage his guilt about deserting the seat. The narrow failure to capture West Derbyshire was made all the more poignant by Walmsley's early death. Some consolation for the party lies in the fact that his widow Joan has gone on to prove one of the Liberal Democrats' strongest parliamentarians in the House of Lords.

Two months after West Derbyshire, there was another near miss, this time against Labour, in Newcastle-under-Lyme, by a margin of 799. There were deep three-way divisions in the Labour camp between the left, the local right-wingers and the party headquarters machine, which an exhausted and cash-strapped Liberal by-election machine did not do enough to exploit.

The Liberal candidate in Newcastle, Alan Thomas, was a CND supporter, a fact which undoubtedly made it harder to squeeze the votes of the Tories, who were trailing a bad third. David Owen argued that the electorate understood that there were differences between the two parties and that they were not affecting support for either of them. An alternative reading suggests that a united merged party could have improved significantly on these by-election performances, winning in both West Derbyshire and Newcastle, and setting a much stronger bandwagon rolling up to the next general election. Nevertheless, there had been advances in local elections. The shire contests in 1985 gave the Alliance the balance of power in twenty-four of the thirty-nine county councils. Over the four years of the Parliament, there was a net gain of over 200 council seats.

This power base in Britain's council chambers was of enormous significance to the Alliance. In the eyes of the electorate, it meant greater visibility and credibility. For the councillors themselves, it led to far more responsibility and professionalism. Andrew Stunell began working professionally for the Association of Liberal Councillors in 1985. He had experienced the advantages and pitfalls of the balance of power in Cheshire, where he was group leader, and had written a booklet called 'Life in the Balance'. He had been impressed by his experience of going in to see the Chief Executive of Cheshire after the 1981 elections and being asked how the party intended to implement one of the key bullet points in the manifesto. Liberal candidates around the country had committed themselves to external efficiency audits. Stunell discovered that nobody had given any thought at all how such an audit would actually be carried out. The policy consisted of no more than the bullet point. From now on, Stunell was determined that Alliance councillors should understand how to get things done and gain a reputation for actually doing them. He recalls explaining that the party should gain the image of being more like the Tories in that respect. It is hard now, he admits, to remember a time when Conservatism was generally equated with practical competence, but that was the case at this point in the 1980s.

As the Parliament moved into its second half, there were many reasons for the Alliance to be cheerful. Both Davids were popular. Opinion poll ratings were strong. Between May 1985 and April 1986, the Alliance averaged 32%, one point ahead of the Conservatives and three points behind Labour.

There were, however, some ominous black clouds on the horizon. The darkest of these was the defence issue. The two parties had established a number of joint commissions on key subjects, of which defence was inevitably going to be the most controversial. The broad outline of the policy was not in doubt. Almost all of the SDP and most of the Liberal Party were opposed to unilateralism, and the membership of the commission reflected a strongly multilateralist approach. It was chaired by a former diplomat, John Edmonds. The key Liberal members were Richard Holme, Christopher Mayhew, Laura Grimond and Paddy Ashdown. None could be called unilateralists, even Ashdown, who had taken a specific line at a specific moment against cruise missiles. The SDP side included Bill Rodgers, John Roper and John Cartwright.

The key question for the commission was over the replacement for Polaris. The decision ultimately was that Britain could afford to postpone the decision. The new Russian President Mikhail Gorbachev had tabled new arms initiatives. Polaris would last until the end of the century. It was entirely plausible to suggest that a firm decision in favour of the Trident weapon could be put off.

At a lunch with Andrew Marr and Martin Dowle of the *Scotsman*, David Steel let slip that the commission would not commit the Alliance to replacing Polaris. The result was the headline 'Owen's hopes dashed'. The story appeared on Friday 16 May 1986. Owen was due to speak at the SDP's conference in Southport the next day. Without consulting any of the SDP members of the commission, he ruled out any compromise on replacing Polaris, thus pre-empting the commission and running roughshod over the policy-making process which had been agreed.

His hard line caused huge ructions in the SDP. Bill Rodgers wrote an article in *The Times* disowning Owen's stance. 'Certainty', he said, 'is not always a virtue. Nor is conviction itself evidence of the truth.' Hugo Young underlined in the *Guardian* the damage that the row could cause to the Alliance's prospects. He warned that it would appear erratic and non-credible: 'This if it happens will have come about because of Dr Owen's determination to be seen as a conviction politician.'

Owen admits in his autobiography that he had not been inclusive enough in his reaction to the *Scotsman* story. Certainly, his uncompromising line, which he repeated in a speech in Bonn to the Anglo-German Society, triggered a reaction from the Liberal Party which did serious damage to the Alliance's prospects. Altogether the defence row was to cost the Liberals and the SDP nine precious opinion poll points.

An attempt was made by the two Davids to patch up their differences by exploring the possibility of a Euro-bomb, based on Anglo-French collaboration. They went together to Paris where they met President Mitterrand and Jacques Chirac, then Prime Minister, and were well received. The idea of strengthening the European pillar of NATO was treated seriously by some commentators like David Watt, the Director of Chatham House, although dismissed by others.

The commission report was duly endorsed by the SDP autumn conference at Harrogate, but when the Liberal assembly debated it in Eastbourne, delegates had in front of them an amendment which approved European co-operation only 'provided that such a defence capacity is non-nuclear'. This amendment was interpreted by the press as unilateralist, although those who supported it denied that it was intended as broadly and most delegates did not belive that they were voting for unilateralism. Two Liberal MPs, Simon Hughes and Michael Meadowcroft, spoke for the amendment. Simon Hughes passionately attacked the concept of 'a Euro nuclear bomb mountain with twelve fingers on the button'. A third MP, Archy Kirkwood, who had co-authored a pamphlet on the subject with Hughes and Meadowcroft, supported them. He says that he was persuaded by the debate that the Euro-bomb was a bad idea, but he admits that part of the motivation of many of the amendment's supporters was the pleasure of sticking two Liberal fingers up at David Owen.

The amendment was carried by 652 votes to 625. Therein lay another irritant for the SDP. The Liberals prided themselves on their party democracy, and delegates to the assembly did have to be democratically elected. Nonetheless, it was not difficult to become a delegate, and it is understandable how some SDP supporters formed the inaccurate impression that anyone could walk off the street and claim a vote. Certainly the activist left had a disproportionate say. The assembly was not truly representative of the membership. The leadership of the day claimed that they were often powerless to influence decisions at assemblies. As David Steel puts it: 'What was damaging was that people could put in amendments scribbled on the back of an envelope the night before to be debated the next day. You never really knew in advance what the issues were. Nor were they necessarily well thought out. You could have rather muddled amendments because the point of view which they were trying to state was not stated very clearly.'

Others protest that the proceedures were not anything like as anarchic as Steel suggests. They put a different interpretation on the Eastbourne debacle. They believe that the leadership was negligent in failing to anticipate the strength of the opposition to the official line. There was no co-ordinated strategy to line up votes in favour of the official line, and some of the speeches on that side were lacklustre, reflecting perhaps a lack of confidence in the Euro-bomb compromise. The defeat certainly came as a surprise. David Steel had toyed with speaking in the defence debate, as he had done in 1984, but he decided that such a move would only have raised the stakes. When it all went wrong, he was at first careful to play the result down as 'a minor irritant', a comment which proved to be a further major irritant to David Owen. By the main evening news, however, Steel was warning that the decision would have to be reversed. Owen was mollified, and resolved to give the other David all the support that he could. Friends believe that the most mortifying part of the episode for David Steel was being patronised by Owen over it.

Simon Hughes remains unrepentant about his role in the drama. He believes that politics is healthier if parties can have genuine open debates at their conferences. What soured the atmosphere, he claims, was not the vote itself but the reaction to the vote. He was certainly left in no doubt about the feelings of his parliamentary colleagues when they met later in the evening of that day. The Chief Whip David Alton and the Isle of Wight MP Steven Ross were particularly sharp with him. He arrived late at the meeting from a fringe event, but not late enough to avoid taking the flak on his own; Meadowcroft (clarinet) and Kirkwood (guitar) were delayed longer because they were playing in a band.

The press certainly saw the vote as a major development. The *Daily Express* headline was 'Ban the bomb vote shatters the Alliance'. *The Times* led with 'Steel defeat puts Alliance in disarray'. At a press conference, David Alton added fuel to the flames by waving the headlines in front of the TV cameras to demonstrate his fury at what the party had done.

In his speech at the end of the assembly, David Steel confronted the anti-nuclear supporters in his ranks head on. He told them that it was totally misguided to believe that the resolution in some way strengthened his hand in manifesto negotiations with David Owen. This was, he said, a breathtaking misjudgement. 'We are either in an alliance or we are not. ... It is unthinkable that we enter the election with two defence and two disarmament policies.' He went on to warn that electoral victory might have been unnecessarily put at risk.

By December, the two leaders were able to launch a joint Alliance statement on defence which made a clear commitment to retaining a minimum nuclear deterrent but did not specify what form the replacement for Polaris should take. But the political damage had been done. The Alliance had dropped nine percentage points in the polls.

As ever, the Alliance's success depended as much on the standing of the other parties as on its own efforts. Neither Labour nor the Conservatives hit the levels of unpopularity which they had suffered in the previous Parliament. The Conservatives could count on a relatively benign economic climate, even though unemployment remained obstinately high. Privatisation was the big idea of their second term and, although their former leader Harold Macmillan, now Earl of Stockton, attacked them for selling the family silver, the policy proved popular. Against this, opposition parties could point to a neglect of the poor and of the public services. The one big crisis which Mrs Thatcher faced was over Westland, when Michael Heseltine became the first minister to walk out of a Cabinet meeting in a hundred years. But the issue at stake was not one which had huge resonance with the electorate at large.

The Labour Party was now under new management. Neil Kinnock had been elected to succeed Michael Foot, and began the painful task of dragging the party back towards the centre ground. A London Weekend Television producer and former party special adviser called Peter Mandelson was hired as Director of Communications. The red rose replaced the red flag. The leadership began to stand up to Militant and other far-left groups.

But Labour was still vulnerable. It was ambivalent about the miners' strike; the unpopularity of the National Union of Mineworkers' Leader Arthur Scargill inevitably rubbed off on the party. Although it dropped its plans to withdraw from the EEC, Labour was still unilateralist. And the leadership could not always control who was selected as parliamentary candidates. All had been well for them at the Fulham by-election, where their candidate Nick Raynsford proved appealing, moderate and highly competent. He gained the seat from the Conservatives, and kept the Alliance candidate Roger Liddle squeezed down in third place.

When in December 1986 the Greenwich seat fell vacant on the death of the Labour MP Guy Barnett, it was a very different story. This time, Labour picked a caricature far-left candidate called Deirdre Wood. She was a gift to the Alliance. She had supported all the most extreme positions available on both the GLC and the Inner London Education Authority. Actions like voting to invite Sinn Fein speakers to speak in London were guaranteed to put off the traditional Labour voters of an area like Greenwich.

The SDP started the campaign well behind in third place. The candidate Rosie Barnes had no expectations of winning. She was looking forward to a month in the limelight before retreating back into obscurity. She underestimated what a formidable campaigner she would be.

For the first time, there was an integrated Alliance campaign. Rosie Barnes was one of the SDP's political virgins. A mother of three children with a job in market research, she had never been a member of a political party until the SDP came along. Alec McGivan for the first time used American techniques for targeting particular groups of voters. The main slogan, however, derived from tried and tested Liberal experience. It read simply 'Rosie Barnes lives here'. A further advantage was that the seat was next door to the one held by John Cartwright, who had a superb constituency organisation. David Owen pulled out all the stops, having cancelled a holiday in India. The Liberals also contributed considerable effort, including the services of two of their most wily campaigners, Chris Rennard and Peter Chegwyn, who wrote many of the leaflets between them.

The mood of the campaign became more and more upbeat. Buttons were distributed, which read 'Say hello to Rosie Barnes'. When Rosie Barnes later became one of the refuseniks who decided not to join the merged party, these were adapted to 'Say goodbye to Rosie Barnes'. In February 1987, however, she was the heroine of the hour. The SDP moved past the Conservatives from third to second place in the polls. Then on polling day, Rosie Barnes had a majority of over 6,000. This was the first time that the SDP had captured a Labour seat.

The result was a great boost to the Alliance. The bandwagon was rolling again, a fact confirmed by the by-election in Truro, which followed Greenwich. David Penhaligon had tragically been killed in a car crash, aged only forty-two. Penhaligon had been a universally popular MP; witty and self-deprecating, he had a strong appeal to people who had little time for conventional politicians. He was a pied piper of politics, with enormous powers of persuasion. His folksy Cornish accent sometimes misled; he had a quick intelligence and an instinctive grasp for political issues. Ever since first being elected he had been in great demand as a media performer, and he was every local party's favourite visiting speaker. Unlike so many politicians, he was also highly numerate.

For the party, there was the consolation of the enormous goodwill and sympathy that followed Penhaligon's death. In the by-election, his twenty-three-year-old researcher Matthew Taylor held the seat with an increased majority and supplanted Charles Kennedy as the youngest MP.

So this time the Alliance was entering a general election campaign on a rising tide. Whereas the two parties had been at around 18% in the first week of the 1983 campaign, they averaged 29% in April 1987 after Truro and obtained 27% of the vote in the May local elections. Labour were on 31% in each poll and, with the track record of Liberal and Alliance progress during general election campaigns, the chances of becoming the second party, at least in terms of popular vote, looked very good indeed.

The SDP and the Liberals believed too that they were in better organisational shape than last time round. They had a joint policy document 'The Time Has Come' agreed and published well ahead of the election. The seat allocations had been worked out amicably. They had a joint Alliance planning group set up to run the election from the centre. The broadcasters had even agreed to parity of air-time with the Conservatives and Labour.

Unhappily, however, the 1987 election broke the mould of third-party general election performances. Far from creeping inexorably up in the polls, the Alliance subsided downwards. They began with a poor first week. The manifesto was given lukewarm notices by the press, even by papers which were reasonably sympathetic, like the *Financial Times* and the *Independent*. The first party election broadcast, a soft-focus production featuring Rosie Barnes and her pet rabbit, was regarded as vacuous. Much of the footage was never intended to appear. The campaign had only discovered on the day of transmission that the broadcast was supposed to be ten rather than five minutes. They hurriedly spliced in material which would have been much better left on the cutting room floor. The Alliance parties also appeared to be attacking the wrong target. Their guns were at first trained very much on the Conservatives, when a much better tactic might well have been to try to push Labour, as the weaker party, aside first.

The biggest problem, however, was the issue of the two Davids. Both did their best to present a common front, to the extent that in the early part of the campaign they did several rather awkward-looking broadcasts side by side with each other. David Steel complained that they looked like Tweedledum and Tweedledee. There was, however, a fundamental problem which neither could disguise. Owen clearly leant towards the Conservatives while Steel leant towards the Labour Party. The press did their best to exploit the difference. The Liberal, Alliance and Liberal Democrat parties have often suffered from the fact that the greatest interest they have for the media is in their positioning vis-à-vis Labour and the Conservatives. With a real possibility in 1987 of the Alliance holding the balance of power, the issue was of obvious importance.

On the Robin Day phone-in on 3 June, David Steel said, 'I would find it unimaginable ... that there would be circumstances in which a minority Government led by Mrs Thatcher could be sustained in office by us.' The next day, David Owen appeared to discount the possibility of the Alliance taking part in a Labour-led Government, saying 'the one fundamental issue for me is the security of our country ... and on that test the Labour Party fails.'

Tom McNally, who was a member of David Owen's campaign team, believes that the Alliance was undermined during the 1987 election by the mobile phone. The journalists on Steel's bus could phone the press on Owen's tour and swap lines to try out on the other leader. The constant probing for cracks in Alliance unity inevitably yielded results. The Alliance headquarters had technology which was supposed to fax information to the buses, but it seldom worked. The media's equipment was much better than that available to the politicians.

The campaign team was headed by John Pardoe. Other members of the inner group included Lord Haris of Greenwich and Polly Toynbee for the SDP and Des Wilson and Paul Tyler for the Liberals. In retrospect, Pardoe says he was the only Liberal that David Owen could bear and the only Liberal who could bear David Owen. Although, with his old Bevanite background, he strongly disagreed with Owen on defence, he regarded him as a genuine radical over issues like welfare and child poverty. From the SDP point of view, Pardoe had the advantage of being clearly independent of Steel. One of Pardoe's main contributions to the campaign was intended to consist of acting as its chief spokesman, which would have been a way round the danger of the two Leaders contradicting each other. The two Davids, however, never properly ceded this role. The campaign team would meet on Sunday nights in the Royal Horseguards Hotel. On the final Sunday, it was agreed that Pardoe would speak to the press, but each David was promptly doorstepped as he left the meeting, leaving Pardoe with nothing left to say.

As always, the Alliance, with most of its main figures fighting tough individual constituency battles around the country, struggled to find personalities to feed the appetites of the London media. One of its mainstays was the Liberal Leader in the House of Lords, the redoubtable Baroness Seear. At one press conference, she was particularly contemptuous of Neil Kinnock. 'They say Mr Kinnock's a nice person,' she said. 'Well, you and I wouldn't employ a cook on the basis that she was a nice person, would we?' The image of each of the reporters at the press conference running domestic establishments with cooks, butlers and housemaids was one to savour.

One candidate who fought the 1987 election recalls that Alliance activists were in denial throughout the campaign. Deep down they knew that there were problems, but they kept telling each other that everything was going very well. Nobody would admit their private fears to anyone else.

In the process of practising this form of mutual self-deception, Liberal and SDP activists on the ground were working very smoothly together. At the centre, however, all was a great deal less smooth. There was not enough co-ordination. Each Leader would have his own advisers who would brief him separately, the two teams only coming together after this process. With Leaders instinctively in sympathy with each other, like Steel and Jenkins, this might have worked. With Steel and Owen, it was a recipe for misunderstandings. David Owen fought the campaign with great verve and tenacity, but he was determined to fight it his own way. The command team at headquarters found it difficult to communicate with him. David Steel appeared much more willing to consult and to accept advice.

Owen acted on the basis that the differences between the two Davids were inevitable; they reflected the fact that they led two parties, not one, and justified his determination to carry on that way. David Steel has claimed that when Owen indicated that he might be prepared to work with Margaret Thatcher, that alienated large numbers of wobbly Labour voters who could have been persuaded to vote for the Alliance. Whichever way, the differences certainly did the campaign no favours.

There was another potential problem with the campaign. David Owen was convinced that it was unrealistic for the Alliance to state that it could become the Government on its own. He persuaded the other key members of the campaign team that it would be a good idea to say that the aim was to achieve the balance of power. The weakness in this argument was that the third party could not determine the relative strength of the other two towards each other. For much of the election, it appeared that the gulf between them was going to be too large for the Alliance to fill. Even though Labour closed the gap in the polls towards the end, the eventual result showed that the balance had been a forlorn dream.

Owen was not fundamentally wrong, however, to break with the tradition that all parties in an election have to claim that they are going to win. In 2001, Charles Kennedy said that his ambition was to win more votes and more seats. He believed that a party that prided itself on honesty should be honest about its expectations, so he made no pretence that the Liberal Democrats were going to win the election. Many of the press regarded the tactic as highly dangerous. Why vote for a party which does not even claim that it can win? But the result showed that the gamble did the Liberal Democrats no harm.

There is another explanation of the poor Alliance performance in 1987 that is equally important. It is that Labour fought an extremely good campaign. Labour's organisation of 1987 was light years away from the shambles of 1983. Peter Mandelson had substituted the red rose for the red flag, and Neil Kinnock was proving a very effective campaigner. The first Labour Party election broadcast, made by the director Hugh Hudson and known popularly as 'Kinnock – the Movie', was an enormous success. The fact that the themes were cribbed from an American election film promoting Ronald Reagan was neither here nor there. The broadcast contrasted particularly favourably with the Alliance's feeble efforts with Rosie Barnes and the rabbit.

Meanwhile, the Conservatives were cruising to victory. They seemed to have luck on their side. On the eve of poll, David Dimbleby asked Margaret Thatcher about the level of unemployment. 'If people just drool and drivel that they care,' she replied, 'I turn round and say, "Right. I'd also like to see what you'd do."' It was a terrible gaffe. If the

Prime Minister had made it twenty-four hours earlier, the Alliance would have had a chance to exploit it. In the event, it came too late in the day to make much difference.

As polling day approached, it was clear that the Alliance campaign had faltered. The *Mail on Sunday*, which had been very supportive up to this point, commented, 'Alas, during this election campaign, the Alliance has shown that it is not yet fit to govern.'

On election day 1987, all hopes of a breakthrough were dashed and the Alliance itself was fatally damaged. In many ways, it was a greater disappointment than 1983. This time, there was no Falklands factor. Some of the wounds at least were self-inflicted. The SDP went down to five seats. Roy Jenkins and Ian Wrigglesworth lost, together with the victor of Portsmouth, Mike Hancock. Neither Shirley Williams in Cambridge nor Bill Rodgers in Milton Keynes succeeded in their bids to return to the House of Commons.

The Liberals were back down to seventeen. They were unable to hold on to their by-election gain in Ryedale. Clement Freud lost in Cambridgeshire North-East. And two seats where MPs were retiring, the Isle of Wight and Colne Valley, slipped out of the party's grasp too. The results suggested that the Liberals remained at least partially a party of outsize local personalities whose votes did not necessarily transfer to their successors.

In compensation, the Liberals picked up three new seats. The QC Menzies Campbell won North East Fife, which contained much of Asquith's old constituency. There had recently still been electors there who could remember walking for two or three hours after work to go and hear Asquith speak at public meetings. But the 'Asquith knew my father' vote was very limited. Regaining the seat was the reward for long years of very hard work over three general elections. Another tireless campaigner, Ronnie Fearn, a long-standing councillor famous for playing pantomime dames at Christmas, gained Southport. And Ray Michie, the daughter of the legendary Scottish Liberal John Bannerman, won Argyll and Bute. There was particular satisfaction in taking this seat off a Conservative MP who had originally defected from the Liberal Party.

Labour had had a disappointing night too. But they could console themselves that they had had a good campaign. They told each other that you need four years to win an election, not just four weeks, and that next time things would be different. The Alliance had already had its 'next time'.

In broader perspective, the result had not actually been that bad for the Alliance. In fact, they had won the second highest popular third-party share of the vote since the 1920s, with an overall percentage share of 23%, 4% better than the earlier near-breakthrough of February 1974. On a pure PR system, they would have had 149 seats in the new Parliament.

A swift recovery might conceivably have been possible. Instead, the parties embarked on a series of actions which brought them down to a level of support lower than the Liberals had enjoyed for most of the 1950s. Having had their greatest opportunity for a breakthrough, they rapidly found themselves instead facing their greatest-ever crisis. John Pardoe describes the events which immediately followed the 1987 election as the worst period of his whole political career, an experience which inoculated him against politics for ever.

At this point in the history of the Alliance, the details of almost every minor episode are disputed by rival participants. In a book about potential breakthrough, rather than about near breakdown, a blow-by-blow account of the rows would be irrelevant. They are worth recording only in order to illustrate the tensions which clearly lay below the surface in the years in which breakthrough was possible, and to help explain the early evolution of the merged party.

The first such factual dispute concerns the question of whether or not David Steel tried to bounce the Alliance into merger in the immediate aftermath of the 1987 general election. David Owen believes that he did. David Steel says that Owen had prior warning, although there had been something of a mix-up over delivering messages.

It is certainly true that Steel was determined to press the case for merger with great urgency, calling for what he called 'democratic fusion' of the two parties the weekend following the general election. He was joined in this desire by three of the four members of the original Gang of Four. All the experience of the previous election campaign told them that this was the right way forward. Bill Rodgers announced his firm view in favour of merger on an election-night TV programme.

Others favoured a halfway house, by which the two parties would remain but would have a single Leader for the next election. This option might have kept more SDP supporters on board, but it would not have solved the problem of duplication of effort and resources. It would have still also allowed the media to exploit any differences between the two parties.

The main opposition to merger came predictably from David Owen. He was originally joined by all the other four SDP MPs. But first Charles Kennedy and then Robert Maclennan broke ranks. This was a defining moment for Charles Kennedy. Still only twenty-seven, he showed considerable courage in standing up against his four older and more experienced colleagues, and in particular facing the wrath of David Owen. When colleagues like Shirley Williams talk about the inner steel hidden by Kennedy's relaxed demeanour, they often cite this seminal moment in his political past.

There had been endless argument on the National Committee about the form of the question which would be put to the membership in the ballot. It was finally agreed that the choice would be:

Option One: Do you want the National Committee to negotiate a closer constitutional framework for the Alliance, short of merger, which preserves the identity of the SDP?

Or Option Two: Do you want the National Committee to negotiate a merger of the SDP and the Liberal Party into one party?

Kennedy became convinced that Option One was not what it seemed, and he asked Owen at the crucial meeting on 29 June whether it could mean eventual merger. When Owen said that it could not, Kennedy announced that he would support Option Two. One of Owen's loyal supporters, Polly Toynbee, denounced him as a traitor. Owen's own attitude was initially calmer towards Kennedy, although the two were to fall out seriously later on.

David Owen's stance was that he did not wish to stop anyone in the SDP who wanted to do so from joining the merged party. At the same time, he did not feel that, even if the majority wanted merger, they were entitled to take away from the minority the right to continue as members of the party that they had joined. Others felt that he was being anti-demo-cratic by refusing to accept the verdict of the majority in a democratic party. His attitude was certainly to lead to enormous acrimony over dividing the assets of the SDP when merger was finally agreed.

There was opposition to merger from within the Liberal Party as well. Since some SDP members felt loath to kill a party which was only six years old, it was not surprising that they had Liberal counterparts who were unhappy about killing a party which was well over a hundred years old.

The two parties duly put the isue of opening merger negotiations to the vote. The Liberal Party made its decision at its autumn assembly in Harrogate. The result was an overwhelming majority (998 to 21). The SDP balloted its membership, which decided in favour by a much narrower margin (25,897 to 19,228). On both sides, there were groups who were determined not to accept the majority verdict and to carry on in their old parties. The difference was that, while Liberals of this view were a small element on the fringe, the SDP refuseniks included the Leader, two of the other five MPs, the two trustees and a narrow majority on the National Committee.

This, moreover, was only the beginning of the troubles which the mergerites were to face. They now had the difficult task of framing a constitution for the new party. Neither the Liberals nor the SDP were short of qualified lawyers, and both parties in addition possessed barrack room lawyers in abundance. Instead of having small negotiating teams, each side had fifteen representatives plus their legal advisers and national secretaries. Negotiations lasted from September 1987 to January 1988. With every day that the talks went on, the merged party that they were to produce was weakened. These negotiations, together with the events which had led up to them and their consequences, were to set the cause of Liberal Democracy back fifteen years. It is only recently that the party has climbed back to the level of support which the Alliance won in the 1987 election.

There were other problems, apart from the structure of the negotiating team, on both sides of the Alliance. The SDP now had a new Leader. When David Owen found himself on the losing side of the merger ballot, he resigned. Robert Maclennan, who had favoured a process of ever-closer union rather than abrupt merger, decided that the only democratic position possible was to accept the verdict of his party. He then, to general surprise, put his name forward for the Leadership and was elected unopposed. He regarded his mission to be to conduct the negotiations sufficiently toughly to preserve the essence of the SDP in the new party. This would avoid a repetition of muddles like the Eastbourne vote, which had happened in the old Liberal Party. It might also convince the anti-mergerites to join the new party after all.

The Liberal team meanwhile included a number of those who had begun their political careers in the Young Liberals, had embraced the cause of community politics and viewed the SDP with the greatest suspicion. Eight of the Liberal members had been directly elected by the Harrogate assembly, and five of them were considered to be potential members of the awkward squad who could not be guaranteed to support

David Steel. Splits within the Liberal negotiating team caused as many problems as divisions between the Liberals and the SDP.

There was much over which they had to argue: the name of the new party; the preamble to the constitution setting out basic philosophy; the question whether there should be a core declaration of policy to accompany the launch and, if so, what it should contain; the degree of centralisation or devolution in the party's structures; the extent to which the conference was to be a sovereign body; the scope for 'one member one vote' ballots; the question whether there should be positive discrimination in favour of women for party posts.

The SDP negotiators wanted to protect themselves against a Liberal take-over, particularly anything which forced them to accept the nostrums of the radical wing of the Liberal Party. That is why they insisted on the policy declaration and why they also wanted the new party's commitment to NATO to be embedded in the preamble to the constitution. They felt, too, that the size of the party conference should be kept down to manageable proportions; they had regarded the old Liberal Assemblies as being essentially self-selecting, which was how embarrassments like the Eastbourne anti-nuclear vote had come about. Their suspicion of Liberal institutions was heightened by the fact that the Liberal Council met during the negotiating process and tried to unpick decisions which the negotiators had already agreed.

The Liberals, not unnaturally, felt strongly about preserving Liberalism. They wanted to resist what they saw as the centralising tendencies of the SDP. They feared the ghost of Dr David Owen hovering over their SDP interlocutors, and suspected the Social Democrats on the negotiating team of tacking rightwards to appease his shade. The greatest difficulties, in fact, were not so much between the negotiators of the respective sides, who established a reasonable rapport with one another. They came from those on the outside, from the anti-merger minorities in both parties.

Every detail was argued with great passion by negotiators on both sides. Their commitment was certainly important for the future of the new party. The problem was that the intricacies of the arguments were of very little consequence to the electorate as a whole. The perception was only of former allies arguing acrimoniously and endlessly over esoteric details. The assumption could reasonably be made that, if these people could not agree amongst themselves, they could not be entrusted with running a Government.

The negotiating process was supposed to be finished by Christmas 1987, in time for special conferences of the two parties in January. In fact, it ground on into the beginning of the New Year. By now, both teams had suffered resignations, John Grant from the SDP side and Michael Meadowcroft from the Liberals.

The last piece of the jigsaw to fall into place was the name. This was the most sensitive of all the questions which the negotiators had to decide. Liberals did not like options like 'The Democrats' or 'Alliance' which lost the word Liberal. The SDP did not like 'Liberal Democrats', which they thought sounded too like a Liberal Party Mark II. 'Liberal and Social Democrats' produced the unfortunate abbreviation LSD. Eventually, they agreed the more unwieldy 'Social and Liberal Democrats', which shortened to the slightly more palatable SLD, inevitably transformed into 'Salads'. This part of the agreement was subsequently to be unstitched, with the result that it was possible over a period of not much more than ten years for the same person to stand for election under four different labels, Liberal, Alliance, SLD and Liberal Democrat, without changing party. It was confusing for the candidates, let alone the electorate.

'Alliance' might have been a better short title to have chosen. Both sides of the negotiating team were prepared to accept it; it was the wider membership of the Liberal Party that disliked it. Some said you might as well call the new party 'Titanic'. But it was a brand name which the electorate knew, and if it had been adopted, it might have made life harder for the breakaway 'continuing SDP' which was later to emerge.

Nevertheless, after the months of wrangling, it seemed that the merger was finally agreed. All that remained was the policy document. This had been entrusted to the two Leaders, David Steel and Robert Maclennan. Steel in turn had largely left its production to Maclennan, who had used the services of two young researchers, Hugo Dixon and Andrew Gilmour, to draft it. They became carried away. Instead of recapitulating existing policy, they came up with some extremely controversial new ideas.

'Voices and Choices for All', as it was called, favoured extending VAT to food, children's clothes, newspapers, domestic fuel and financial services. It also endorsed the Trident missile and advocated continuing the civil nuclear-power programme. During most of the document's gestation, David Steel was in Kenya. He returned only in time to read it through while tired from his trip, and pronounced himself satisfied. One of the controversies over this period concerns the extent to which Steel had delegated supervision of the document to his Deputy Alan Beith during his absence.

A press conference had been organised to announce the details of the merger. Neither members of the negotiating team nor Liberal MPs had had a chance to see it until the day before. Slowly it began to dawn on them that it was a document which they would find completely unacceptable. Steel was informed of this in no uncertain terms at a meeting of the Liberal Policy Committee, with the press conference a mere eighteen hours away. With Maclennan's reluctant consent, a group met into the early hours of the morning to attempt a redraft.

Meanwhile, the original had been given to the press. The morning newspapers presented it in dramatic terms and senior Liberals decided that a redraft was not going to work. The whole document had to be withdrawn. Steel told Maclennan the bad news at 11 a.m., with less than an hour to go to the press conference.

Both Leaders knew that their positions were on the line. After much agonising, they decided to postpone the press conference. The journalists were not only already waiting but had also, unfortunately, been given the original document. It had gone to several leader-writers as well some time earlier. When the two Leaders' aides, Alec McGivan for Steel and Simon Coates for Maclennan, arrived in the room, it was too late to withdraw it.

The subsequent meeting of the parliamentarians was extremely traumatic. Both leaders were under great stress. Maclennan was in tears at times. At one moment, the Liberals feared that he would head for the door to go and announce that the deal was off. Simon Hughes and Malcolm Bruce guarded each of the two exits physically to restrain him. David Steel, too, was clearly under great pressure. At one point, Nancy Seear, never much of a 'touchy feely' kind of person, put her hand on his knee to steady his nerves.

Ultimately, the two Leaders agreed to start again with a completely different document based on the 1987 manifesto. David Steel described 'Voices and Choices' in the terms of the famous Monty Python sketch as a 'dead parrot'. But the damage had been done. The new party was to be created in the most inauspicious circumstances.

With the merger agreed, Robert Maclennan set off on another mission. He took Charles Kennedy down to see David Owen in an eleventh-hour attempt to persuade him to come into the fold of the merged party. Maclennan planned to point out that both the constitution and the preliminary policy stance of the new party were so close to those of the SDP that there was no logical reason for him not to join it. Although Maclennan knew that there was little chance of Owen agreeing, he felt it important to make the attempt. Owen duly gave his two former colleagues a curt brush-off, and refused to come to the door to say anything to the TV cameras.

The question remains whether Owen could conceivably have become Leader of the merged party if he had agreed to join it. Although there was strong antipathy to him amongst many senior members of both the SDP and the Liberals, he was still very popular in the country, and grass-roots activists recognised his abilities as a vote-winner. A few Liberals, like Des Wilson, tried to persuade Owen that he had a good chance of winning.

The last act in the merger drama took place at the parties' two special conferences. The Liberals met in Blackpool on 23 January and approved the deal overwhelmingly, by 2,099 to 385. The SDP met in Sheffield. With David Owen advising his supporters to abstain, merger was voted through by 273 to 28, with 47 registering their abstention. Subsequently both parties balloted their memberships, which endorsed merger but on low turnouts.

It had been a bruising period. Rather than maximising the combined strength of the two parties, there was a danger that the merger process had weakened and undermined it. Nonetheless, the infant party had underlying strengths which derived from both its parents. Its structures draw as much on the SDP as on the Liberal model. This made it considerably less unwieldy and anarchic. The Liberal Democrats are considerably more than a Liberal Party Mark II. Several of the new MPs elected in 1997 were former members of the SDP, including Mark Oaten, Vince Cable, Evan Harris and Paul Burstow. The SDP victor of the 1984 Portsmouth by-election, Mike Hancock, was finally returned to the Commons as well. In the House of Lords, the Liberal Democrat Leadership has passed between former members of the Gang of Four, from Roy Jenkins to Bill Rodgers to Shirley Williams. The party has had three former Social Democrat Presidents: Ian Wrigglesworth, Charles Kennedy and Robert Maclennan; now it has a former Social Democrat Leader. The SDP could reasonably echo Mark Twain in saying that reports of its death in 1988 were greatly exaggerated.

The charge is sometimes laid against the SDP that it was responsible for prolonging the period of Conservative Government in the 1980s and 1990s. The large Tory majorities of 1983 and 1987 were obtained with far less than 50% of the national vote. If the SDP had not fragmented the anti-Conservative vote, things might have been very different. Alternatively, it is argued that if the Gang of Four had stayed inside the Labour Party, the era of New Labour would have dawned a great deal earlier and the party would have made itself more electable much faster.

The opposite can just as easily be argued. In 1983, there was no way in which the country would have elected a Labour Government led by Michael Foot standing on a programme of unilateralism, withdrawal from Europe and extensive nationalisation. The founders of the SDP had done their best within the Labour Party to overturn that agenda and they had failed. The shadow of the 1983 Labour programme still lay heavily over Labour in 1987. The Conservatives were always going to beat Labour in those elections. The only difference that the Alliance could have made would have been to deprive them of an overall majority. Equally, the creation of the SDP may have hastened rather than retarded the creation of New Labour. The defections had a shock effect which, in time, proved very salutary.

The bizarre element in retrospect is that so many of those who drove the SDP's leaders out of the Labour Party because of their far-left views went on to sustain the popularity of the Liberal Democrats because of their right-wing behaviour in Government. Among those who have gone well past the old SDP on their long march away from socialism are Alan Milburn, Stephen Byers and David Blunkett.

Back in 1988, it was left to the new merged party to begin its own long march back to political credibility.

7 From Parrot to Project, 1988–99

Having disposed of the parrot, the new party was in great need of a phoenix – the disputes after the 1987 election appeared to have left very little more than ashes. A chance for a fresh start came with the Leadership election of 1988. Before his fatal car crash, David Penhaligon had been the frontrunner for the succession. The eventual victor Paddy Ashdown reckons that Penhaligon would have been a very formidable candidate. He would have stood against him, but he thinks that he would have lost. After his death, a number of names were in the frame, but the eventual contest was fought between only two MPs: Ashdown and Alan Beith. Nonetheless, the differences between their platforms gave the party a clearer choice than either the Pardoe–Steel contest of 1976 or the Ashdown succession race of 1999.

Alan Beith was the better-known quantity. An MP since 1973, he had stood in for David Steel during his sabbatical in 1983. He was the candidate for continuity. He wanted to preserve as much as possible of the old Liberal Party in its successor. Paddy Ashdown represented much more of a gamble. Only in Parliament since 1983, he had attracted suspicion from some colleagues through his obvious ambition to lead the party. The media frequently tipped him for the role as well.

Ashdown promised leadership from the front; Beith guaranteed more consultation and consensus.

Although both Beith and Ashdown had been Liberal MPs, Ashdown was the clear favourite with the SDP. Tom McNally was a key member of his campaign team and he was endorsed by Roy Jenkins, Shirley Williams and Bill Rodgers. The Ashdowns were invited to Roy Jenkins' house at East Hendred to be appraised over Sunday lunch. Paddy Ashdown remembers it as 'a daunting experience, only alleviated by some very nice champagne before lunch and some excellent claret during it.' Roy Jenkins says in his autobiography, 'We did not know him well, and he was politically inexperienced to be a leader. So it was not a choice without risks.'

Ashdown's literature was in colour, and Beith's in black and white. It was all part of the contrast between the two. Ashdown's backers set out to excite the membership, spending £25,000 on what was, by Liberal standards, a very glitzy campaign. The candidate was presented as someone who would modernise and professionalise the party. Beith's backers saw Ashdown as a bit too flashy.

For the most part, the contest was conducted in a gentlemanly fashion. Beith rapidly disowned a document put out by one of his supporters listing fifteen reasons not to vote for Ashdown. An embarrassed Liberal MP, Alex Carlile, appeared on *Newsnight* to discuss the document, while refusing to confirm that he was the author. Later, a ploy by another Beith supporter backfired. He had submitted examples of the handwriting of the two candidates to a graphologist for analysis. The result showed that Ashdown had much stronger leadership qualities.

There was one issue on which Paddy Ashdown has admitted that he was wrong and that Alan Beith was right. This was the question of the short name by which the party was to be known. It was obvious that 'Social and Liberal Democrats' was too much of a mouthful to be used on all occasions. Ashdown favoured 'the Democrats' for short, a description which appealed to former members of the SDP; Beith championed the title 'Liberal Democrats'. When Ashdown won, he put all the authority of his mandate behind persuading the Conference to endorse 'Democrats', which it agreed by the relatively narrow margin of 650 to 500. The decision was only reversed after the setbacks of 1989.

Alan Beith believes that dropping the word 'Liberal' trampled on the members' feelings of self-worth. It also meant many more months of time-consuming dispute within the ranks of the new party, which led to further derision from the outside world. The implication was clear: if the party could not even agree on its own name, it was hard to take it very seriously on any other issue. Paddy Ashdown concedes in retrospect that championing 'The Democrats' was the biggest mistake of his leadership: 'I completely failed to understand that hearts run parties as well as heads. You could not ask people to divorce themselves from a tradition in which their heart was absolutely steeped, the tradition of Liberalism.'

Paddy Ashdown won comfortably, by a margin of 71.9% to 28.1%. In many ways, the new Leader was atypical of the party from which he came. He had had a career in the Royal Marines, in the Foreign Office and, less publicly, in British intelligence. The Liberals had not experienced the firm smack of military discipline since the days of Colonel Frank Byers. They needed it. It was good for them.

One of Ashdown's closest allies of this period, Richard Holme, describes him as a platoon commander who behaved in a text-book fashion towards a demoralised army. He knew how to rally his troops. Although he did not have long experience at Westminster, Ashdown had spent years as a Liberal activist. The Liberals had been a poor third in Yeovil when he was selected, and he had won the seat by the classic strategy of grass-roots campaigning.

Ashdown's background was on balance a great asset, but there were disadvantages. Less immersed in the ways of the party at national level – or at least of the old Liberal Party – than Alan Beith, he faced a steep learning curve. Another Ashdown ally, Archy Kirkwood, believes that the new leader lost out by not consulting Alan Beith more in the early years of his Leadership. It is perhaps in the nature of politics that leadership contenders find it difficult to close ranks once the contest is over.

In retrospect, Alan Beith takes a generous view of Ashdown's Leadership. He believes that his military ways and his technique for setting clear objectives, which he then set out to achieve, were of great benefit to the party.

Right from the start, Paddy Ashdown began pursuing what became known as 'The Project'. He believes that, fundamentally, this was not anything new. It was a question of continuing to pursue the goal at which Jo Grimond, Jeremy Thorpe and David Steel had all aimed – the realignment of the left. At times, this has been conceived as a plan to supplant Labour as the opposition to the Conservatives. At others, it has been a question of working with likeminded people within the Labour Party. Variations in the strategy have depended far more on the state of the Labour Party than on the state of the Liberals or Liberal Democrats. It is only in very recent years that the strategy has lost relevance, as the Labour Party has begun to occupy so much ground which traditionally belonged to the Conservative Party.

Unlike David Steel, Ashdown had a great interest in the detail of policy. Here he wanted the Liberal Democrats to strike out in new directions. He regarded the old policies of the Alliance as too corporatist. He was keener on market solutions, with a new emphasis on small business, competition and enterprise. Ashdown decided personally to chair the Federal Policy Committee, which became the engine room of policy development in the new party. Charles Kennedy continued the tradition when he became Leader.

There are times when parties need warriors as their leaders and times when they need healers. Ashdown was not just a warrior; he was profesionally trained to kill. He was the right leader for the time. Without him, the new party could easily have run into the sand. He was a worrier as well as a warrior. His diaries are full of forebodings about the future of the party and his own strategy for it. Those close to him became used to early-morning summonses to discuss the latest crisis. Yet, although he sometimes exasperated his lieutenants, Paddy Ashdown had a gift for inspiring them and commanding their total loyalty.

He took over a party in dire straits. It was to sink to a level at which its standing in the polls included 0% within the margin of error. It was heavily in debt, and the bailiffs were never far away. A demoralised staff was facing inevitable redundancies. When Ashdown went over to pose outside the Cowley Street headquarters for the cameras after his victory in the Leadership election, he knew that inside the building there were people from the PAYE department of the Inland Revenue looking for assets to distrain because the party had fallen behind with its payments. Eventually they were persuaded to give the party more time to pay, on the grounds that there was nothing of sufficient worth to distrain.

The party had accumulated a deficit of £600,000. The main reason was the big drop in membership, particularly amongst former SDP members. The people who were most disillusioned were those who had not belonged to a party before and had seen the Social Democrats as a fresh force in politics set to break the mould. As one senior SDP survivor puts it, 'Theirs was the rational decision to take; those of us who soldiered on were the ones acting irrationally.' Eventually, as a result of a great many painful redundancies, the deficit was reduced to a manageable £70,000.

The first political battle was to knock out the Owenites. Two by-elections, at Epping and Richmond in Yorkshire, would have made invaluable platforms for the launch of the new party. Labour was not fully reformed. Mrs Thatcher was increasingly past her zenith. Instead, the Social and Liberal Democrats found themselves entering the lists in competition with the so-called continuing SDP. At Epping in December 1988, the SLD candidate came second with 8,879, with the SDP on

4,077. Between them, they had more votes than Steve Norris, the victorious Conservative, did. Then at Richmond in February 1989, the SDP were second with 16,909, with the SLD on 11,589. The Tory victor here, William Hague, had only 19,543. A single Alliance candidate would have taken the seat comfortably and held back the political ambitions of a future Conservative Leader.

It was a bad moment for the new party. Further overtures were made to David Owen which went nowhere. The local elections in May 1999 were not the disaster that had been feared, but the European election in June that year was a humiliation. The Greens surged past the SLD to take 15% of the vote against 6%. The party had only one second place anywhere in the country. The new Campaigns Director Chris Rennard had based himself for most of the campaign in Plymouth and Cornwall, realising that this was the only real prospect for success.

On the night, I was in a BBC studio with Russell Johnston, who felt, as many Liberals did that night, that the cause for which he had fought all his life was in ruins. Paddy Ashdown wrote in his diary that he was 'plagued by the nightmare that the party that started with Gladstone will end with Ashdown'. In the Commons, Ashdown had been regularly subjected to the same offputting tactics from the other parties which his predecessors had suffered. In the wake of the European elections, the Labour MP Tony Banks heckled, 'Bite the capsule, Paddy.'

However, having hit rock bottom, Liberal Democrat fortunes began to improve. For a start, the name question was finally settled; following a ballot of members in the autumn, the party would now be called the 'Liberal Democrats'. Secondly, the party began to mark out some clear policy positions. The old argument over defence was settled decisively at the 1989 conference. After strong speeches from Menzies Campbell, Laura Grimond and Chris Walmsley, the delegates voted by a margin of two to one against unilateralism. Thirdly, Paddy Ashdown began to make a real impact on the national stage. The issue of Hong Kong played to his strengths. He was a Mandarin-speaker and knew a great deal about China. More importantly, he was speaking up for a clearly Liberal principle, the right of admission into the UK for British passport holders after the atrocity of Tienanmin Square.

The cause which Ashdown chose to champion was not a particularly popular one. Nonetheless, as well as displaying real principle, it did have political advantages. It gave the leader a much-needed high profile. Even those who disagreed with him gained respect for his courage and knowledge of the subject. By December 1989, the new party had scaled the dizzy heights of 9% in the polls.

July 1990 finally saw the end of the destructive battle with the continuing SDP. The Liberal Democrats, who had been throwing their limited resources at pushing the Owenites off the battlefield, finally achieved their objective at a by-election in Bootle. The SDP candidate polled only 155 votes, just a third of the tally that went to Screaming Lord Sutch of the Monster Raving Loony Party. The *Sun* reported the story with a caricature of Owen wearing Sutch's trademark top hat with the line 'Owen's in sutch a state because he can't even beat the loonies'. The National Committee of the SDP decided it was time to fold its tent. Most of the remaining Owenite troops disappeared from the political scene, although some made welcome additions to the ranks of the Liberal Democrats.

There was also a continuing Liberal Party candidate at Bootle, who received substantial financial backing from a disgruntled party donor. This threat was seen off too. Furthermore, the Greens were rapidly proving to have been a nine-day wonder. They were much damaged by the claims of one of their highest-profile figures, the sports commentator David Icke, to be the Son of God. Liberals may have made wild statements in their time, but Icke was in a class of his own.

Having cleared these challengers out of the way, the Liberal Democrats at last had a real opportunity to make a significant electoral impact. The MP for Eastbourne, Ian Gow, was blown up by the IRA.

The constituency was one in which the Liberals had traditionally polled strongly. Paddy Ashdown's first instinct, nonetheless, was to give the Conservatives a free run. He felt that it was distasteful to become the beneficiaries of a terrorist outrage.

The new party's Director of Campaigns Chris Rennard had imbibed the street-fighting Liberal activism of his native Liverpool with his mother's milk. He was not going to let an opportunity like this go by. He wrote Ashdown a memo in which he stated that he was appalled at the idea that the party might not fight Eastbourne: 'It will not be seen to be bold and courageous', the memo said, 'it will make you a laughing stock in Walworth Road, Downing Street and eventually in the quality press that you threw away this chance.'

Ashdown was persuaded and the party threw all its resources at the by-election. Strangely, *Old Moore's Almanack* had predicted that the Liberal Democrats would win a by-election on 18 October 1990, the very day that was set for the Eastbourne poll. The newspaper which the party produced for the voters had a column by 'Eastbourne's resident stargazer', one Chris Rennard by name, who predicted that a Liberal Democrat victory was in the stars.

And so it seemed. The Liberal Democrat candidate David Bellotti went on to win the by-election with a majority of 4,500. There had been a gap of three years since the last Alliance by-election gain. The indefatigable BBC Political Editor John Cole had gone to bed before the result in the clear expectation that there would be no upset. Eastbourne was a sign that normal service had resumed; the by-election machine was back on track. The campaign team drank their hotel dry of champagne. There remained the much higher hurdle of converting by-election wins into substantial general election gains, but at least the party was back in the race. The national poll rating went from 8% to 18% almost overnight.

Ashdown's military experience was to stand him in good stead again during the 1991 Gulf War. He gained further recognition on radio and television as a result of his obvious expertise. There was some initial reluctance in the party to back the Government on the issue, but the parliamentary party all eventually came into line.

That year saw further electoral gains. Ribble Valley fell to Mike Carr within a week of the end of the Gulf War. This was another champagne moment, but unfortunately supplies in the Clitheroe hotel where campaigners were celebrating proved inadequate and the off licences were long since shut. Gerald Vernon-Jackson, who had helped mastermind the Liberal Democrat victory, had a brainwave. He ascertained that surplus stocks remained in the Conservative Club, walked in there, suggested that they might not find much call for champagne that night and negotiated the purchase of a case.

The local branch of the bookmakers Joe Coral had been offering odds of six to one against a Liberal Democrat victory at the beginning of the campaign. On the day after the result, a long queue of party supporters had to wait outside for the betting shop to open. Coral's had to phone for a special delivery of extra cash before it could let its jubilant customers in.

Then in the local elections, the Liberal Democrats gained 520 seats, substantially more than Labour. Finally in November, Nicol Stephen, subsequently a Cabinet minister in the Scottish Executive, won the Tory seat of Kincardine and Deeside. After Eastbourne, the Tory Chairman Kenneth Baker commented that the parrot had twitched. Now it was spreading its wings energetically and blowing loud raspberries at the Conservative Party.

Just as the 1992 general election campaign was getting under way, a new and unexpected development threatened the revival. The newspapers had got hold of a story that Paddy Ashdown had had an affair with his former PA Tricia Howard. Details of this episode had been kept in the safe of his solicitor Andrew Phillips, from which there had been a robbery. Initially, the party attempted to stop publication by serving an injunction. When this strategy looked like failing, Ashdown took the brave decision to break the story himself at a press conference. The tactic worked. It earned him the nickname from the *Sun* of 'Paddy Pantsdown' but it also resulted in an increase in support for the party in the polls.

Nevertheless, 1992 was inevitably going to be a survival election. The Liberal Democrats had avoided meltdown, but they were not in a position yet for a breakthrough. At least they did not have the problem of two Leaders with two teams and two headquarters. There was no ambiguity about who was in charge of the campaign. It was run by the former Liberal Party President Des Wilson, who kept in close touch with the Leader. Privately, the aims were realistic, but modest. The party aspired to hold on to its existing seats, to enhance Paddy Ashdown's reputation and to be seen to be running a professional campaign.

After all the traumas of the past five years, this was the most which could reasonably have been achieved. The eventual result saw a drop in the percentage share of the vote from 1987 by four and a half points, but a net gain, disregarding by-elections, of one seat. The three seats won at by-elections – Eastbourne, Ribble Valley and Kincardine and Deeside – went back to the Conservatives. But there were four gains: by Paul Tyler in North Cornwall, Nick Harvey in North Devon, Don Foster in Bath and Nigel Jones in Cheltenham. The Bath victory knocked the Conservative Party Chairman Chris Patten out of Parliament. Furthermore, Cyril Smith broke with the track record of previous retiring Liberal MPs by successfully handing his Rochdale seat on to a Liberal Democrat successor – Liz Lynne, a speech consultant and former actress who had once appeared in *The Mousetrap*. Russell Johnston achieved the feat of holding his seat with the lowest ever percentage share for a winning candidate. In Inverness East, the votes split almost equally four ways, with Sir Russell squeaking home on 26%.

The Liberal Democrats emerged from the campaign with more members and in much better heart. Paddy Ashdown and Des Wilson had reason to be satisfied.

The most innovative aspect of the Liberal Democrat campaign was the plan to put a penny on income tax to improve education, a policy which had been agreed at the 1991 party conference. The first half of the election campaign was dominated by the issue of tax, with the Conservatives launching repeated broadsides against what they called Labour's tax bombshell and, with the support of the Conservative press, shooting sizeable holes in John Smith's Labour shadow Budget. So the penny on income tax was high risk, and there were some in Liberal Democrat ranks who believed that it was a mistake.

Nevertheless, there is no evidence that the penny damaged Liberal Democrat prospects. It had the advantage of giving the party a distinctive policy of honesty in taxation. More than in previous elections, there was a Liberal Democrat pledge which voters could readily recall. In the past, surveys had shown that the electorate found it difficult to remember any specific policies of the Liberals or the Alliance. Furthermore, in 1992 Labour looked as if they would put taxes up a great deal more than the Liberal Democrats would. The penny sounded very modest in comparison with the unspecified tax rises which John Smith and Neil Kinnock were believed to be planning.

Meanwhile, the new Leader was proving a success on the stump. The *Guardian* had already praised the manifesto as outdistancing its competitors 'with a fizz of ideas and an absence of fudge'. Towards the end of the campaign, the paper commented, 'Mr Ashdown is the only winner of this campaign. The movement and the arguments have all come from the Liberal Democrats. They are the movers and the shakers.'

Until the last week, the Liberal Democrats seemed set for a better result than the one which they actually obtained. The downturn in support was much more to do with the Labour Party than with the Liberal Democrat campaign itself. Having alienated many voters with their tax policies and their triumphalism, Labour started talking positively about constitutional change and sharing power.

A week from polling day, Neil Kinnock offered the Liberal Democrats what he called 'a place at the negotiating table in discussions over whether Britain should have a new electoral system.' Paddy Ashdown said that the offer was little better than 'wobbling on the fence'. Although the Conservatives had ruled out PR, he predicted that they too would consider it if the electoral arithmetic led to a hung Parliament. The issue, he said, 'puts us right at the centre of the election'.

The Tories, however, saw this tentative courtship between their two opponents as an opportunity. John Major says in his autobiography, 'It made the pair look like trimmers prepared to scrabble for whatever bit of power they could get.' The Conservatives began to turn their fire on the Liberal Democrats as well as on Labour. On the final Sunday of the campaign, John Major, who had dubbed PR as 'Paddy's Roundabout', made his celebrated 'Wake up' speech, which spelt out his view of the dangers of constitutional reform.

Then the next day, the Tories devoted their press conference to the dangers of electoral reform. Douglas Hurd, the Foreign Secretary, warned that a hung Parliament would 'hang the recovery, paralyse business decisions and smother consumer confidence'. He went on, 'To expect the Liberals to control Labour would be like asking Dad's Army to control the Mongol hordes.' The Home Secretary Kenneth Baker went much further over the top. Citing the recent success of Italian and German parties of the far right, he claimed 'Proportional representation has helped the Fascists to march again in Europe. It is a terrible warning to us about what could happen if we threw away our system of first past the post elections ... If PR turned out to have the same results, it could be a pact with the devil.'

When the election was over, one of the key Tory strategists, John Wakeham, described the Conservatives' pleasure at being able to 'line up their two targets and shoot them with one bullet'. The Conservatives had been helped by the fact that their Director of Communications, Sean Woodward, overheard the entire Labour general election strategy being outlined by his counterpart David Hill to Roy Hattersley – he had a fortuitously close table to them at a London restaurant.

The Tory tactic had some effect. For the Liberal Democrat campaign, it was a distraction. Instead of concentrating the voters' minds on the core issues of health and education, where the party's policies had great appeal, the issue was whether the Liberal Democrats would let in a Labour Government, a spectre which frightened many of the floating voters who were vacillating between the Liberal Democrats and the Conservatives. Thanks to his performance at the party's rally in Sheffield, where he sounded more like an over-enthusiastic rugby supporter than a Prime Minister in waiting, the prospect of Neil Kinnock in Number 10 frightened many voters a great deal more than the idea of John Major staying on. And the Tories managed to convince many of the floaters that the Liberal Democrats would put Kinnock in. John Major accused Paddy Ashdown of being 'the doorkeeper to a Labour Britain'.

Paddy Ashdown feels now that he and Des Wilson did make mistakes in the last week of the 1992 campaign. They wanted to be centre stage and on the issue of a hung Parliament from the Sunday onwards. And it was exactly as they had planned. Ashdown says:

> My interviews that Sunday were overly swaggering (I have viewed them since). I used words like 'don't even pick up the phone if you won't talk PR'. Major was saying, 'Wake up Britain – don't sleepwalk into constitutional instability.' This was an old Tory trick they always play – so we should have been

aware of it. Major's was the right line and in tune with the
public's fears and mine was the wrong one. We had underesti-
mated the Kinnock factor. I was seen as opening the door of
Number 10 for him. This awoke all the fears of a return to
1974. The Sheffield rally did the rest.

In constituencies like Hazel Grove, the effect of all this was deadly. The candidate Andrew Stunell was a veteran campaigner with an unerring instinct for the direction in which the electoral wind was blowing. During the final weekend of the campaign, he was convinced that he was well ahead. But he found the last few days before polling day the most miserable that he had ever encountered on the stump. On doorstep after doorstep, he felt his lead melting away. Many voters mentioned the Sheffield rally, and their fear of seeing Neil Kinnock in Number 10. Stunell's difficulties were compounded by the same local problem which Shirley Williams had encountered during the Crosby by-election. The Society for the Protection of the Unborn Child had distributed leaflets against him in every Catholic Church on the Sunday before polling day. He ended up losing by 929 votes; he had expected the margin to be worse.

In the final week of the campaign, Paddy Ashdown did his best to return to the party's positive messages. At a rally in Bath, he said:

These are the issues which this election should have been about.
About the opportunity for education, and our responsibility to
fund it adequately. About the need for new skills, to deal with
the new technologies and the new, competitive world. About
individual rights, and equality of opportunity. About the threat
of pollution, and the measures we can take to deal with it now.
About our future in Europe, which must not be pushed to one
side. And about the quality of our democracy, and how we raise

its standards. That is what this election should have been about. Not about the bickering and the insults, but about the future, and what it means.

Without the Sheffield rally and the Tory onslaught against PR, the Liberal Democrats might have ended up holding the balance of power from the beginning of the 1992 Parliament. They nearly achieved this result anyway. If only 1% of the votes had been cast differently, the Conservatives would have been without an overall majority.

Had they wanted to do so, the Liberal Democrats would have found it hard to avoid the final days of the campaign being dominated by constitutional reform. They suffered the problem that they have always faced at elections: they are very seldom able to set the agenda themselves, and are obliged instead to respond to the issues raised by the other parties. Nonetheless, a lesson was learnt. The 1997 and 2001 Liberal Democrat general election campaigns put the issue of fair votes firmly on the back burner.

In 1992, to the surprise of most of the commentators and pollsters, the Conservatives had won a fourth term of office and, despite the narrowness of their victory, there was talk of them becoming a permanent party of government. One obvious explanation of this Tory hegemony was that they faced a divided opposition. Even in the 1983 landslide, Margaret Thatcher had won far less than 50% of the votes cast.

That inevitably set non-Conservatives thinking afresh about how the Tories could be removed. Paddy Ashdown had always been uncomfortable with the concept of equidistance, which held that there was nothing to choose between the Conservatives and the Labour Party. It had made sense perhaps in 1983, when Labour were for unilateralism, nationalisation and withdrawing from the European Union. By 1992, Labour were at least halfway towards their subsequent Blairite identity.

Paddy Ashdown made his formal break with equidistance in a speech in the Guildhall in Chard in his constituency on 9 May 1992. In language drawing on ideas which had gone through numerous drafts and caused fierce debate in the parliamentary party, he argued that the Liberal Democrats needed to 'work with others to assemble the ideas around which a non-socialist alternative to the Conservatives can be constructed'. He referred to what he called Labour's 'careful and coded words about consensus' and expressed the hope that they represented 'a shift of historic importance for the whole of British politics, and one which Liberal Democrats should welcome . . . Our contribution, if it is to be successful, must reach out beyond the limits of our own party. Our role is to be the catalyst, the gathering point for a broad movement dedicated to winning the battle of ideas which will give Britain an electable alternative to Conservative government.'

The timing of the speech meant that it was seen as a hand-grenade lobbed into the contest to succeed Neil Kinnock as Leader of the Labour Party. It helped make the story front-page news, at least for the more sympathetic broadsheets. The *Observer* described it as 'the first tentative steps towards an informal alliance with Labour'. The lead story in the *Independent on Sunday* was headlined 'Ashdown swings to Labour'.

The main interest, however, was in the reaction from Labour politicians. All treated the move with caution. The warmest welcome came from Robin Cook, who was acting as John Smith's campaign manager. He said that he accepted Paddy Ashdown's recognition that 'we are likely to be better in opposition if we do it together'. Smith's rival Bryan Gould called the proposals 'interesting', and the Employment Spokesman Tony Blair suggested that, while the party was against pacts and confident that it could win on its own, it was not opposed to a 'dialogue of ideas'.

Outright opposition came from predictable quarters. Margaret Beckett said that she could do without being patronised by Paddy

Ashdown and accused him of 'hubris'. John Prescott commented that Paddy Ashdown's dreams had been decisively rejected by the electorate. And for good measure Ken Livingstone called on the left to vote against any candidate who favoured relations with the Liberal Democrats.

The speech caused great ructions in Liberal Democrat ranks at all levels. Those most opposed tended to be people for whom the main opposition was Labour rather than the Conservatives. In the parliamentary party, the strongest criticism came from Liz Lynne, the new MP for Rochdale, and from Simon Hughes. Paddy Ashdown also had robust critics in the Association of Liberal Democrat Councillors, of whom a large element represented council seats in northern cities which would otherwise be Labour. At the 1992 autumn conference at Harrogate, a move for closer links with Labour was decisively rejected, although Ashdown's supporters managed to get a resolution through which did not completely tie the Leader's hands.

The issue continued to cause tensions throughout the rest of the Parliament. There were times when Ashdown appeared ready to put his Leadership on the line over it. The most significant step forward he was able to achieve was at the 1995 conference, where the party formally abandoned equidistance. In practice, this meant that coalition with the Conservatives was ruled out. It did not mean that coalition with Labour was ruled in.

There were two events during the 1992–7 Parliament which had a more profound effect on the prospects of the Liberal Democrats than any strategic decisions which the party might make for itself. The first was Black Wednesday, when the pound fell out of the Exchange Rate Mechanism. From that moment onwards, the Conservative Party lost its ace card. It was no longer seen as the party of economic competence. All talk of Britain turning into a one-party Conservative state evaporated. It was clear that the Government was on the ropes. Eleven years later, Black Wednesday stands out as a watershed of enormous importance. The Conservatives have never sustained any durable lead in the national opinion polls since that time. If it proves ultimately that the Conservatives were a party in permanent decline, the beginning of the end will be dated back to 16 September 1992.

The second event was the death of John Smith in 1994 and the election of Tony Blair to succeed him. Until then, Labour were still tarred with the failures of the 1992 campaign. John Smith was an enormously decent man and a strong performer in the Commons, but he did not represent the clear break with the past embodied by Tony Blair and New Labour. Nor, as far as the Liberal Democrats were concerned, did he have the same interest in dialogue which Tony Blair was to show.

The period between Black Wednesday and the death of John Smith saw a great opportunity for the Liberal Democrats. The party traditionally suffered in periods between elections from lack of media attention. With only twenty MPs, a small professional press office and no national newspapers officially supporting the party, it was very difficult to persuade the journalists to cover what the Liberal Democrats were saying. The only time when they could guarantee attention was during a by-election campaign.

The party was lucky with the seats which happened to fall vacant. The first was a completely unexpected contest. Judith Chaplin was a high-flying new Conservative MP, who had gone into hospital for a minor operation and tragically died. It was a seat where the Liberal Democrats had a presence in local government. The candidate, David Rendel, was well known locally and had fought strongly in 1992, coming second. The seat had not, however, been on the target list and it was far from being a pushover. Judith Chaplin's majority was over 12,000.

The Liberal Democrats benefited, however, from Conservative mistakes. The local Tory party passed over both a competent local standard-bearer and a high-flyer who had lost his seat at the 1992 election in favour of a rather overweight outsider from Somerset called Julian Davidson. The media by-election circus unkindly dubbed him

'Mr Blobby'. For the Liberal Democrats, Chris Rennard moved into the constituency to mastermind the campaign. It focused on the issue of VAT on fuel, which had been introduced in the March Budget, and ruthlessly exploited the unpopularity of the Chancellor, Norman Lamont. Much use was made of targeting, with messages carefully tailored to different sections of the electorate.

Paddy Ashdown made frequent visits to Newbury to lead the charge into Tory territory. The military metaphors, which feature so prominently in the reporting of electoral contests, tripped easily off his ex-marine tongue. He told a press conference that this was a 'battle royal'.

Towards the end of the campaign, Chris Rennard deployed another of his well-honed skills. He managed to depress expectations so that the media were led to believe that this was a tight contest. The body language of the supporters who gathered for the count at Newbury race-course suggested otherwise. Paddy Ashdown describes in his diary how he was woken at 4.20 a.m. by the General Secretary, Graham Elson, who told him that David Rendel had got in by 22,000. Ashdown said he wanted to know the majority, not the total vote. 'Paddy, that is the majority,' said Elson.

The press gave the Liberal Democrats credit for the triumph. It had coincided with local election results which gave the party 381 gains. *The Times* called the outcome for the Conservatives the 'most calamitous electoral showing for decades' and a superb night for the Liberal Democrats. The paper noted that the Liberal Democrat surge had come earlier than in previous Parliaments. But it observed that the opposition to the Government remained divided.

One consequence of Newbury was the resignation of the Chancellor of the Exchequer Norman Lamont, three weeks after the result. Paddy Ashdown called it the beginning of the end to John Major's Premiership. The Liberal Democrats were now ahead of the Tories in the opinion polls, on 27% to the Conservatives' 24%.

The next by-election arose in a seat which was far safer for the Conservatives than Newbury had been – Christchurch was considered rock-solid Tory territory. The late MP Robert Adley had had a majority of 23,000. This time, the Conservatives picked a competent candidate, Robert Hayward, who was a former MP. But the Government was in deep trouble. The effects of the recession were still biting. VAT on domestic fuel remained highly unpopular. There was a widespread perception that public services had suffered under the Conservatives. Furthermore, there was a huge internal battle raging within the Government over the ratification of the Maastricht Treaty. Paddy Ashdown said during the campaign that the virulent contagion of the Tory civil war had reached into the heart of the Cabinet and was paralysing the Government.

The Liberal Democrat candidate was Diana Maddock, a councillor from Southampton. The campaign machine swung behind her, proving itself particularly successful in squeezing the Labour vote, which shrunk from 7,000 to fewer than 1,500 on the night. In this 'true blue' Tory area, a new campaigning technique was added to the repertoire. Selected constituents were invited to tea parties with Liberal Democrat peers. There were so many volunteers in the campaign that it was possible to deliver a campaign newspaper to every household within a single day by 4 p.m. The result was the biggest swing against a governing party in history, of over 35%. The Liberal Democrat majority was over 16,000.

A measure of the demoralisation of the Government was that Central Office had written off the chances of victory well before polling day. Over the Parliament, the Tories were to go on to lose every single one of the eight by-elections in the seats which they had held, four to the Liberal Democrats, three to Labour and one to the Scottish Nationalists. In retrospect, the only question was over which of the opposition parties stood to gain the most.

Relations between the Liberal Democrats and Labour remained edgy.

The Liberal Democrats had angered the Labour Party by supporting the Government on the key votes on Maastricht at the end of 1992. There were some within the Lib Dems' own ranks who thought that Paddy Ashdown was wrong to pass up the chance of defeating the Government. Given the number of rebels on the Tory side, John Major needed Liberal Democrat votes to get the legislation through.

Paddy Ashdown was determined for the party to stand on principle by its European credentials. His argument was that, where the issue at stake was Britain's future in Europe, the party should vote in favour, but where it became simply a question of the Government's survival, it should vote against. Some of the parliamentary party, however, were uneasy with this line, and there was a great deal of pressure from the grass roots of the party. One MP, Nick Harvey, who had declared against Maastricht during the election campaign, maintained his opposition throughout the course of the Maastricht debates and voted accordingly. In the key votes in December 1992, the Government only won because of Liberal Democrat support. The Labour Party was furious. Paddy Ashdown was branded as a traitor.

The party's stance on Maastricht put down an important marker. Although the Liberal Democrats did attract a great deal of flak at the time, the signal that it sent was that they were not simply in Labour's pocket and that they were prepared to stand by their fundamental principles.

The party also set out a policy on Maastricht which was internally more controversial. The Liberal Democrats came down in favour of a referendum on the issue, making it clear at the same time that they would campaign for a 'yes' vote. Older MPs like David Steel and Russell Johnston opposed the move. The younger generation, in particular Charles Kennedy as the spokesman on Europe, believed that politicians had a duty to go out and explain the European cause to the electorate; where there was a significant constitutional issue at stake, it was right to have a referendum. The party's MPs in the end took the significant step of dividing the House on a Liberal Democrat opposition supply day in favour of a referendum.

Certainly the Newbury and Christchurch by-elections demonstrated that supporting the Government on Maastricht had not done the party any lasting damage. In 1994, a third promising vacancy arose. The Conservative MP for Eastleigh, Stephen Milligan, died in embarrassing circumstances. Given the dire state of the Government, the big question was whether Labour or the Liberal Democrats would be the main beneficiaries of the Conservatives' unpopularity. In the event, David Chidgey won the seat for the Liberal Democrats by an impressive 9,000 majority. Labour came second.

The same night, Labour polled very well in the Euro-elections, with the result that they not only won a number of seats in London, the Midlands and the North, but also deprived the Liberal Democrats of gains which they could have made in the South. The party was close behind the Tories in seven seats, including Devon, where it was robbed of victory by a spoiler candidate who styled himself as a 'Literal Democrat'. There were only two actual gains: in Cornwall and Somerset. It was a step forward for the party to have won its first ever European seats, but a disappointment nonetheless to have missed so narrowly in so many others.

The Euro-elections took place in the middle of the Labour contest to succeed John Smith. Soon, though, Tony Blair had won that election and the Liberal Democrats had to contend with the phenomenon of Blairism. For some people, Tony Blair appeared to be achieving the aims for which the SDP was originally founded. He was weaning his party away from socialism and creating the kind of social democratic party that the Gang of Four had envisaged back in 1981. A few prominent Liberal Democrats were to defect to New Labour, including Roger Liddle, Andrew Adonis, David Marquand and John Dickie. Furthermore, the three members of the Gang of Four who were active in the Liberal Democrats all had warm words for the new Labour Leader. Roy Jenkins called him 'the most exciting Labour choice since the election of Hugh Gaitskell'. Shirley Williams suggested that the two parties should work together towards a common programme. Bill Rodgers said that he hoped Blair won the next election and that there could be a coalition based on mutual tolerance. The *Observer* had a headline which read 'Gang Show for Blair'.

Tony Blair's election effectively ended any hope of the type of breakthrough which had been mooted in Liberal and Liberal Democrat circles for the past quarter-century. From now on, there was very unlikely to be any prospect of the Liberal Democrats overtaking Labour to be the main opposition to the Conservatives. In 1993 and 1994, the party was regularly scoring in the mid-twenties. By the start of the 1997 campaign, the rating had slipped to below 10% in one poll and not much more in the others. The party continued to perform well in local elections. By 1996, it had more councillors in Britain as a whole than the Conservatives did. But there was long experience of council votes not translating into parliamentary votes, and no great reason to suppose that the trend would change.

The euphoria for Tony Blair was to last up to the 1997 election and beyond. It was a dilemma for the Liberal Democrats; it was as if a new tidal wave had hit British politics. As Alan Leaman, one of Paddy Ashdown's closest advisers, saw the dilemma, it was a question of being swamped by the tidal wave or trying to surf it and seeing how far it took the party up the beach. Paddy Ashdown chose the latter option, and it proved, as he had promised, to be a bumpy ride. But it also promised a breakthrough of another kind – the chance to form a coalition with Labour and to achieve proportional representation.

The strategy was based on the special relationship which Ashdown had begun to develop with Tony Blair before he succeeded John Smith and went on to pursue apace once Blair had become Leader. They had come into the House of Commons at the same election in 1983 and, despite an age gap of twelve years, got on extremely well together. One of Paddy Ashdown's favourite themes was his opposition to tribal politics. He regarded Tony Blair as a leader who had not come originally from the Labour tribe, and who was not nearly as deeply committed to it as his predecessors. Tony Blair, meanwhile, was formulating the belief that the rift between the Liberals and the Labour Party at the beginning of the twentieth century had been a tragic mistake which had allowed the right to dominate politics far longer than it should have done. He professed a historic mission to heal the divide.

The courtship between Ashdown and Blair lasted for five years. The path of true love did not, however, run at all smoothly. Elements of their respective political families regarded each other with rather less enthusiasm than the Montagues felt for the Capulets. Large sections of the Labour Party, including senior figures like John Prescott, Jack Straw and Margaret Beckett, wanted to have as little to do with the Liberal Democrats as possible. Equally there were many in the Liberal Democrats who felt a positive revulsion for the Labour Party. The opponents of the strategy included some of the parliamentarians and many of the councillors, who wielded great influence in the party.

Paddy Ashdown's method of retaining support for his plans was to build up huge amounts of credit in the bank with the party activists, which he would then spend when he really needed to do so. He now enjoyed considerable status as the party Leader. He was popular in the country and regarded as courageous by the membership for speaking out on behalf of Liberal causes. He was also extremely energetic in campaigning with activists around the country. He was therefore able, from time to time, to persuade the party to do things that it did not really want to do.

The Project, as it became known, never went as far as Paddy Ashdown had wished. He and Tony Blair had discussed the possibility of an election campaign in which there were agreed policies between the two parties on key issues to be followed and coalition after the result. Some progress was made, but there were many stumbling blocks, chief among them being Tony Blair's agnosticism over PR.

Several of the talks took place in the house of Tony Blair's former pupil master Derry Irvine, who had an extensive collection of modern painting. Key Ashdown allies including Archy Kirkwood, Richard Holme and Bob Maclennan would go along to discuss the details with leading Labour figures. One participant has a vivid memory of Robin Cook's head framed in the legs of a nude in the painting on the wall behind him.

Before the 1997 election, the most tangible result of the talks was the Cook–Maclennan Committee, which was set up to discuss issues of mutual constitutional interest. The establishment of a Scottish Parliament had already been agreed in separate talks in Scotland under the Scottish Constitutional Convention. Cook–Maclennan agreed to enshrine the European Convention on Human Rights into the British constitution, to introduce PR for European elections, to set up a commission on voting reform for Westminster and to reform the House of Lords. The agreement was a significant moment. Now that for the first time rival parties had agreed ahead of an election on a series of wide-ranging reforms, it seemed as if the old political system was capable of changing after all.

There is a great deal of unfinished business still from the Cook–Maclennan agenda. But the Liberal Democrats can at least claim the credit for achieving a very significant proportion of its objectives. In terms of making the party relevant to the governance of Britain, Cook–Maclennan can certainly count as a breakthrough.

Tony Blair had told Paddy Ashdown that he would contemplate a coalition with the Liberal Democrats even in the event of obtaining an overall majority. He saw the value of having allies in the Government who were likely to be a great deal more sympathetic than the left of his own party. The result of the election produced a majority which was so large that the new Prime Minister did not need the Liberal Democrats. Even the day after polling day, there seemed a chance that he might nonetheless include Liberal Democrat ministers. But he would have faced formidable opposition from the Labour Party if he had done so.

Paddy Ashdown walked a tightrope in the run-up to the election. He wanted to remain sufficiently friendly to Labour to put maximum pressure on the Tories and to keep open the possibility of a deal with Tony Blair. On the other hand, he needed to keep the separate and distinct identity of the party. The Liberal Democrats could not win the seats where they were second to the Conservatives if they were seen to be too close to Labour.

Key lieutenants like Chris Rennard found themselves constantly pushing the Leader to be tougher on Labour. They believed that the party had to learn from the lessons of 1992, when former Conservative supporters were deterred from voting Liberal Democrat because they felt the party was too tied to Labour. The roughest period between the two parties was the Littleborough and Saddleworth by-election in 1995. The late MP Geoffrey Dickens had been a Conservative, but it was clear that the race was going to be between Labour and the Liberal Democrats. The Liberal Democrats had been a clear second last time, and they believed that their candidate Chris Davies was the rightful challenger to the Tories. But Labour selected a tough street-fighter called Phil Woolas, and sent Peter Mandelson up as his principal minder. The campaign became pretty vicious and personal. Davies took a very progressive line on the drugs issue, and was repeatedly attacked on this by his Labour opponent. The result was a narrow victory for the Liberal Democrats, and a long memory of bad blood in the North West.

Davies was not the only further addition to the Liberal Democrat parliamentary party. Two Conservative MPs crossed the floor to the party, after long cloak-and-dagger negotiations. The first was the high-profile Devon MP Emma Nicholson. The negotiations with her were a triumph of Ashdown's tradecraft. The coup was planned with meticulous care and the Leader put great emphasis on the need for split-second timing. The neighbouring MP Nick Harvey played a key role too. As the deadline approached, pager messages to him from Ashdown became ever more insistent, culminating in a command to 'drop everything' just as he was having his inside leg measured for a new suit by an attractive saleslady in Austin Reed.

With the announcement due on the BBC *Nine O'Clock News* on 29 December 1995, Harvey's staff were deputed to visit the homes of the leading officials of Emma Nicholson's local Conservative Association at precisely 20:55 hours. They were to put a letter through the letter-box explaining her decision and to ring the bell or kick a milk bottle to ensure that the householder was alerted. On no account were they to remain on the doorstep to be confronted, but this way the local Conservatives could not complain that they heard the news first on the television. The rest of the world, including the media, was duly taken completely by surprise. It was the lead story on the BBC and continued to feature in the news for several days. Ashdown's advisers had persuaded him that his original idea of making the announcement on New Year's Eve would have had much less impact.

The second defector was the Bolton MP Peter Thurnham, who made the transition in two stages, first to Independent then to Liberal Democrat. Following his decision, the Parliamentary Party was up to twenty-six, six more than at the beginning of the Parliament.

For all these successes, the Liberal Democrats entered the 1997 general election campaign barely into double figures in the opinion polls. With Labour's huge lead, there was not much press interest in the possibility of a hung Parliament. Consequently, aside from the by-election and the defections, little attention had been paid to the party. The limelight was monopolised by Tony Blair.

Nonetheless, Chris Rennard and the campaign Chair Richard Holme had a plan for ruthless targeting of winnable seats. Starting two years before the election, Rennard laid down stringent targets which candidates would have to meet in these seats in order to qualify for money from the centre. They were obliged to deliver a certain number of editions of a party newspaper round their constituency and to contact a given percentage of the electorate. They also had to attend a number of training weekends.

Money was, as always, tight. In 1996, an offer came from the owner of Harrods, Mohammed Al Fayed, of £50,000 for party funds. It was tempting. As the Chairman of the Finance Committee of the time, Tim Clement-Jones, points out, 'There were not many people lining up to stuff our mouths with gold.' However, the party had the good sense to turn the offer down.

With very few exceptions, the target seats were all constituencies held by the Conservatives, which Labour stood no chance of winning. There were no formal pacts, but the *Daily Mirror* had been primed to advise its readers how to vote tactically to ensure the defeat of the Conservatives. The Liberal Democrats believed that they could make substantial gains, taking their total number of seats well into the thirties.

The polling evidence in the run-up to the general election was less encouraging. Gallup on 23 March 1997 put the Liberal Democrats on 10%. On 6 April, they were down a further point to 9% in a survey by MORI. The media had been treating New Labour as the only opposition act in town. The Liberal Democrats had been starved of press and TV coverage.

Nevertheless, Tony Blair had taken New Labour so far to the right that there was a new space on the political spectrum for the Liberal Democrats. Scarred by their experiences of the shadow Budget in 1992,

New Labour pledged not to raise income tax. The Liberal Democrats stuck to their policy of a penny for education. Paddy Ashdown described their programme as a 'tax covenant with the voters', and it was given the seal of approval of the Institute for Fiscal Studies, which confirmed that its figures added up.

The Liberal Democrats drew their own lessons from their 1992 campaign. Remembering the damage that the row over constitutional change had caused five years before, they decided to stick firmly to the issues which most engaged the voters. Campaigners were given the acronym CHEESE. It stood for Crime, Health, Education, Economy, Sleaze and Environment.

The 'S-word', Sleaze, was an issue which helped both Labour and the Liberal Democrats. In one constituency, Tatton, previously one of the safest of all Conservative seats, they both agreed to stand down in favour of the independent, Martin Bell, in order to unseat Neil Hamilton, who was accused of taking money from Mohammed Al Fayed in brown paper envelopes.

Despite the co-operation with Labour of the past few months, the Liberal Democrat campaign kept its distance from Millbank Tower. The campaign reverted to an old Liberal and Alliance theme. Its first broadcast depicted Labour and the Conservatives as Punch and Judy, attacking them for negative campaigning. There was substance in the charge. Each had accused the other of lying over pensions. The Conservatives had accused Labour of planning to absorb Britain into a federal Europe. Labour had accused the Conservatives of planning to destroy the National Health Service. The electorate responded well to a party which appeared to be appealing to the electorate in less strident tones and to be emphasising the positive aspects of its own proposals.

As the campaign progressed, the enormous Labour lead began to be reduced. The votes were not transferring to the Conservatives, but to the Liberal Democrats. Paddy Ashdown's party rose from 9% in the polls to

19%. The actual result at the ballot box was slightly short of this. Overall, the percentage nationally was down on 1992. But this time the targeting strategy had worked triumphantly well. The Liberal Democrat vote was up 4% in the seats which were targeted and fell by 2.3% in the seats which were not.

The haul of seats exceeded all expectations. On polling day, the campaign chair Richard Holme estimated that the party would win between thirty-five and thirty-seven seats. The final total was forty-six. Where in the past there had been numerous near misses, this time there were several gains by incredibly narrow margins. Edward Davey in Kingston had a majority of fifty-six, Adrian Sanders won Torbay by twelve and Mark Oaten made electoral history by winning Winchester by a majority of two.

Oaten's result was not declared until after 6 p.m. the day after the election. The returning officer allowed the parties to appoint fresh scrutineers, and one of the Liberal Democrats' most experienced agents, Candy Piercy, was parachuted down to Winchester in time for the restart of the count at 2 p.m. on the Friday afternoon. She took the precaution of telephoning the party's lawyers to confirm that a crucial change had taken place in election law. If a voter put a cross from corner to corner, right over the entire ballot paper, and the two lines happened to intersect in the square allotted to a particular candidate, it had previously counted as a vote for that candidate. The new rule disallowed such votes. On the final recount, it emerged that the returning officer had allowed two votes on this basis to the Conservatives. In a *coup de théâtre*, the Liberal Democrats produced a fax of the relevant page of the new legislation. It made all the difference.

Many of the new MPs were in Parliament through sheer perseverance. Donald Gorrie was elected in Edinburgh West at his fifth attempt at the age of sixty-four. It was also fifth time lucky for Andrew Stunell in Hazel Grove. Mike Hancock returned in Portsmouth South after an absence of ten years from the House. There were also new members with solid professional experience outside politics. Three of the new MPs were medical doctors: Peter Brand, Evan Harris and Jenny Tonge. Phil Willis had been Head of a tough comprehensive in Leeds. Vince Cable had been Chief Economist for Shell International. Professor Steve Webb of Bath University was one of the few acknowledged experts on the welfare system. At the same time, the new parliamentary party had a lower average age than both Labour and the Conservatives. Seventeen of the MPs were under forty. These were not people who would be content to remain marginalised in a third party for the whole of their political careers.

The most significant change, perhaps, was that the new MPs knew that they had not been elected simply because of their outstanding personalities and their profile locally. They were in Parliament because they were Liberal Democrats. The new parliamentary party could be fractious on occasions, like its predecessors. On the whole, however, it showed far more self-discipline than the MPs had displayed in the past. The parliamentarians developed the habit of having sharp debates in private, but then accepting the view of the majority once it had been decided. The Conservatives used to boast that unity was the Tory secret weapon. It was clear now that the Liberal Democrats had taken it from them.

There were still weaknesses in the make-up of the parliamentary party. There were no ethnic-minority representatives in its ranks, and only three women. It was unlucky that two of the three seats that the party lost in 1997 had both been held by women: Liz Lynne's in Rochdale and Diana Maddock's in Christchurch. Labour had operated a system of women-only shortlists, which had been ruled unlawful, but only after a great many women had been selected. The Liberal Democrats looked old-fashioned in comparison with the ranks of 'Blair Babes' opposite them. The party has subsequently made numerous attempts to address the problem. Majority opinion believes that overt positive discrimination is illiberal. Instead a gender balance task-force has been working to encourage women to put themselves forward for selection, and to help them succeed in selection contests. The battle is far from won either for women or for ethnic minorities. At least in Lord Dholakia, elected President of the Party in 2000 the Liberal Democrats can boast the most senior ethnic minority representative in British politics.

The 1997 result was a triumph for the Liberal Democrats, who now had more MPs than at any time since 1929. It was a tribute, in particular, to Paddy Ashdown, who had picked the party off the floor when he was first elected Leader nine years before. In a way, 1997 was a real breakthrough. Having forty-six MPs meant being far more visible in Parliament and in many more parts of the country. In another sense, however, the party's clout was less than it might have been. Had the Labour majority been narrow, the Liberal Democrats would have been able to wield great influence. After such a huge landslide to the Labour Party, it was much harder for them to make the difference which their campaign slogan had promised.

The 1997 election saw another change which made a great difference to the Liberal Democrats. They negotiated a large increase in their share of the so-called Short money, the resources paid out of public funds to assist opposition parties in Parliament. With five times the kitty which it had had before the election, the party was able to fund a team of senior researchers, specialising in the main portfolio areas, who helped to give the MPs a great deal of extra impact in Parliament.

Paddy Ashdown had talked in great detail to Tony Blair about the possibility of coalition. On polling day on 1 May, while visiting a school in Taunton, Ashdown took a call from the Labour Leader. Blair had sounded keen on bringing the Liberal Democrats into Government even if he won a large majority. The day after polling day, the new Prime Minister had cooled. The two Leaders discussed instead the idea of a joint Cabinet committee on which Liberal Democrats would sit, a plan that had first been mooted in the Liberal Democrats' contingency planning for a hung Parliament in 1992.

The Liberal Democrats announced that their policy towards Labour was to be one of constructive opposition. This was firmly in line with the rejection of adversarial politics which the Liberal Democrats and their predecessor parties had espoused for decades. It was a common-sense approach, a question of supporting the Government when the party agreed with what it was doing and opposing it when it disagreed.

Paddy Ashdown still wanted to take the relationship further. He believed that the way to make the Liberal Democrats relevant for the future was to establish a joint programme in Government with Labour. It was vital that this was not simply a Labour Government with a few Liberal Democrat ministers. The most essential element would have been the acceptance of PR by the Labour Party. Ashdown said that he did not want office for himself; he would remain party Leader, with senior Liberal Democrats like Menzies Campbell and Alan Beith in the Cabinet.

So, while the meetings of the new Joint Cabinet Committee were announced publicly, Paddy Ashdown was meeting Tony Blair privately to work towards what he called 'TFM', The Full Monty, named after the successful film of that name. Ashdown would report back regularly to an inner group of advisers. Almost all of them were more cautious about The Project than he was. Equally, they agreed that there was sense in exploring what Labour might have to offer.

The Joint Cabinet Committee undoubtedly delivered results. Its existence was one of the reasons that New Labour was prepared to devote so much time in its first years in office to constitutional reform. Compared with those of the Lib–Lab pact of the 1970s, its achievements were substantial. Labour would probably have enacted Scottish and Welsh devolution anyway, but the cause of proportional representation for European elections was very much in the balance, given the opposition to it in the House of Lords, and the JCC made the difference. In addition, the Government enacted limited Lords reform, gave the Liberal Democrats a fairer proportion of peerages and introduced at least a measure of freedom of information.

The Full Monty, however, depended on a clear promise of proportional representation for Westminster. The Government appointed Roy Jenkins to head a commission on electoral reform. Once it reported, Paddy Ashdown needed a firm commitment from the Government that there would be a referendum on the issue and an indication from Tony Blair that he would campaign for a 'yes' vote. Roy Jenkins's report, published in October 1998, struck a subtle balance. It compromised between the convictions of the PR purists and what the Labour Government might be prepared to accept. The solution was a system of AV-plus, which aimed for broad proportionality while preserving the link between individual members and their constituencies.

The Jenkins Report broke the mould of such documents by being written in colourful and often witty language. He described the 1997 election as the Labour Party 'after many thirsty years, having a cornucopia of luscious psephological fruit emptied over its head', while the Single Transferable Vote was compared to 'a caricature of an over-zealous American waiter' insistent on offering more choices than people actually wanted. For all the report's seductive style, however, the Government was to push it into the long grass, a decision which ultimately killed The Project.

Paddy Ashdown devoted great efforts to keeping The Project on the road in the face of considerable opposition within the party. Simon Hughes, now a senior MP, was amongst the leading sceptics; in his constituency, Labour was the enemy, and his activists were strongly against continuing the relationship with the Government.

Charles Kennedy was known to have doubts too. At the spring conference at Southport in March 1998, Ashdown's allies averted a move to rule out coalition with Labour. The party did, however, bind the Leader into a double lock, which ensured that the parliamentary party and the conference were consulted before there was any coalition agreement.

In the late autumn of the year, after some ambiguous but mildly encouraging words from Number 10 on proportional representation, Ashdown announced that he had agreed with Tony Blair to expand the scope of the Joint Cabinet Committee. He faced a series of extremely acrimonious meetings, first at the parliamentary party, then at the Federal Executive and finally at the Federal Policy Committee. The outrage was particularly directed at the idea that people were being bounced. As Paddy Ashdown admits himself, a great deal of bouncing was taking place. This was simply the only way in which he could achieve his objective. It meant him spending his hard-earned political capital heavily at the key meetings, but in the end he got what he wanted.

However, although the remit of the Joint Cabinet Committee was expanded, it was to achieve relatively little more. The truth was that there were too many people in the Cabinet who were opposed to co-operation with the Liberal Democrats. Those from the party who were involved differ in their estimation of the extent to which Tony Blair himself was committed to The Project. Some believe that he entertained it only as an insurance policy against a small majority or trouble with his own left wing. Others think that he was serious about it, but only as a means to swallow the Liberal Democrats up and prevent the party from being an irritant. Many were disappointed that the Prime Minister let the issue of PR for Westminster languish for so long.

Paddy Ashdown has a theory about the Prime Minister's decision-making processes which he describes as 'Zen-Blairism'. He believes that

Tony Blair will do nothing for ages, waiting for the constellations to settle around him before making a move. PR for Westminster just never seemed to be in the stars during the Ashdown leadership.

In many other ways, Tony Blair proved a disappointment to the Liberal Democrats. In his speech at the 1998 autumn conference in Brighton, Paddy Ashdown posed the question whether Blair was a pluralist or a control freak. As time has gone on, the verdict has come down more and more on the control-freak side. There were some reasons to give New Labour a fair wind in its first year. Apart from its constitutional programme, the Government gave independence to the Bank of England, a policy which was in the Liberal Democrat manifesto but not that of Labour. But there were many negative points to be put into the balance, in particular the decision to starve schools and hospitals of resources by sticking to the Conservatives' spending plans and a succession of illiberal measures on penal policy.

The Project belongs on the list of near breakthroughs which did not come off, although it was different in nature from previous near misses. If coalition had been offered and accepted, it would have caused great ructions in the party. If, however, it had guaranteed proportional representation for Westminster, the Liberal Democrats would probably have accepted it.

Paddy Ashdown believes that there are naturally five main parties in British politics, a nationalistic party of the hard right, a Christian Democrat party, the Liberal Democrats, New Labour and the real socialists. If there is PR, the old parties could easily break up into their natural constituent parts, and coalitions are likely to be formed by different combinations of the five resulting political forces. Politics in many continental countries functions in this way. There may still come a time when Britain follows suit.

It was entirely logical to go on exploring the relationship with the Labour Party. Although The Project did not succeed in its final objectives, there were considerable advantages to be derived from its pursuit. In time, the scope for further benefit diminished, and the Labour Government distanced itself increasingly further from Liberal Democrat philosophy. The change in the relationship which evolved after the Ashdown era was far less to do with a change of direction on the part of the Liberal Democrat leadership, and far more a product of the evolution of the Labour Party in the wrong direction.

There were reassuring signs that, while some in the party may have had their doubts about The Project, the electorate as a whole felt favourably towards the idea of constructive opposition – a BBC poll showed a majority in favour. The policy was clear at the time of the first by-election of the new Parliament, which was a triumph for the Liberal Democrats. The Conservative loser in Winchester, Gerry Malone, had challenged the result. The outcome of the rerun in November 1997 was a Liberal Democrat majority for Mark Oaten of 21,000.

There were other signs of progress. More former Conservatives began to come over to the Liberal Democrats. In the aftermath of the 1997 general election, the former Tory MPs Hugh Dykes and Keith Raffan together with an ex-MEP, Peter Price, joined the party. In 1998, another former MP, Anna McCurley, followed their example, together with a sitting Conservative MEP, James Moorhouse, who timed his move to coincide with the Conservative Party conference. The local elections in 1998 delivered the great prize of control of Liverpool City Council to the party. In the following year, the Liberal Democrats picked up Sheffield and Stockport as well. By the end of the Ashdown years, the Liberal Democrats held nearly 4,500 council seats, compared with the tally at the end of the Alliance era of 3,220.

In January 1999, Paddy Ashdown announced that he was stepping down from the Leadership. He had been in his exhausting and often thankless job for eleven years and The Project appeared to have run out of steam. Ashdown wanted to take his career in new directions while he was still young enough. He had told Tony Blair before the election that he intended to stand down during the following Parliament. In different circumstances, nevertheless, he might have been persuaded to stay on. Some of his allies are convinced that he would have ended up as a minister himself in any coalition, and that once in office he would not have wanted to give up.

Ashdown decided to give the party notice of the decision rather than go straight away. He wanted to stay in post to see the Liberal Democrats through the important elections for the Scottish Parliament, the Welsh Assembly and the European Parliament. Equally, he did not want to have to keep lying when people asked him whether he was planning to step down.

There was some anxiety in the party whether it would be a handicap to have a lame-duck Leader. In the event, the strategy did no discernible harm. Ashdown could take pride in the fact that he was leaving office at a time of his own choosing, and bequeathing the party to his successor in a very healthy state. There was a huge contrast both with the legacy that he himself had inherited and with the situation in which his predecessor David Steel had found himself when first elected.

The Scottish and Welsh contests were of great importance to the Liberal Democrats. They could say that they were the first of the main parties to champion the cause of devolution, and the only one really to believe in the idea. The Conservatives were against it; the nationalists saw it only as a stepping stone to independence; and the Labour Party was only in favour so long as the Governments in Edinburgh and Cardiff did the same as the Government in London.

The other great significance that these elections had was that they were fought under proportional representation. The party had fought for the principle for years, but the practice proved challenging. The Liberal Democrat success at the 1997 general election had been based on a strategy of ruthless targeting. In a PR election, all constituencies must be covered; every vote counts. In both Scotland and Wales, the party set great store by the second 'top-up' vote. Since the Labour Party was likely to win more 'first past the post' seats than its proportion of the votes warranted, a Labour vote in the top-up seats was a wasted vote. The hope was that support would go to the Liberal Democrats instead.

In the event, that proved too complicated a message to get across to the electorate. The Liberal Democrats actually performed better in the 'first past the post' element of the contest than they did in the second vote. They held all the seats which they had won in the 1997 election, and picked up one more in both Scotland and Wales, Aberdeen South and Cardiff Central. The final tally was more than respectable, with seventeen Scottish seats and six Welsh ones.

All the same, the complexities of the electoral system gave some of the candidates anxious moments. David Steel, who was a list candidate, was one of the last to be elected. Having championed proportional representation for his entire political career, he wondered fleetingly during the interminable wait for his result whether PR was all that it was cracked up to be.

These elections were very much a matter for the Scottish and Welsh parties, though Paddy Ashdown did make visits to both countries. At the Scottish conference in Aberdeen in the run-up to the campaign, Ashdown visited an air-sea rescue centre with Jim Wallace. The two took part in an exercise which involved Ashdown reverting to his Marine persona and diving into the water to 'save' Wallace. It was probably the best photo opportunity which the party had ever staged, but Wallace vowed that in the forthcoming leadership election he would vote for any candidate who guaranteed not to make him go up anything or down anything which looked dangerous.

The elections proved a learning experience in other ways. In Scotland, it was obvious that there was likely to be a coalition Government. Liberal Democrat spokesmen were constantly being asked which policies were or were not negotiable. In one interview, the leader Jim

Wallace was trapped into saying that the abolition of student tuition fees fell into the non-negotiable category.

The party ended up with the balance of power in both Scotland and Wales. The Scots, following the strategy which had been agreed before the election, went into negotiations with the largest party, Labour. In retrospect, they believe that they did not allow enough time for the talks. On the continent, several weeks can elapse before a Government is formed. Some of the new members of the Scottish Parliament took considerable persuading before they agreed to the deal which emerged. When all the other MSPs had agreed to it after a tense meeting, one announced that he would have to consult a number of people in his constituency. He was firmly told that he could have half an hour to make a couple of phone calls.

Tony Blair, meanwhile, had repeatedly been on the phone to Paddy Ashdown, asking him to bring his troops into line. Ashdown had to explain to him how devolution works. The decision was a matter for the Scots.

As the Parliament developed, the partnership government was to stand the Liberal Democrats in very good stead. Jim Wallace, as Deputy First Minister and Justice Minister, gained a far higher profile than any Scottish Liberal Democrat had had before. Although he was derided at first by the Scottish press, his standing went steadily up during the Parliament's first term. He ended up acting as First Minister for three separate periods: during Donald Dewar's illness, after his death, and after the resignation of his successor Henry Macleish. The Scottish Liberal Democrats succeeded in securing the abolition of tuition fees and in establishing free personal care for the elderly. It was an achievement to which the UK party could point with pride.

Another result of the Scottish election was the election of David Steel as Presiding Officer of the new Parliament. Having chaired the convention which agreed the form which the Parliament should take, he was the natural choice. The Presiding Officer in Edinburgh does not have to cut himself off from his party quite as definitively as the Speaker at Westminster. The result was that there were two David Steels. North of the border, there was Sir David Steel, who was strictly non-partisan. South of the border he metamorphosed into Lord Steel of Aikwood, the Liberal Democrat peer.

David Steel was not the only Liberal Democrat presiding officer in the UK. The Northern Ireland Assembly in Stormont was chaired by John Alderdice, the former leader of the Alliance Party who was also a Liberal Democrat peer. And a third peer, Sally Hamwee, was to become co-chair of the Greater London Assembly. It was tempting to put a sign over the Cowley Street headquarters saying 'Liberal Democrat Party: by appointment, suppliers of presiding officers to Her Majesty the Queen'.

In Wales, Labour decided to form a minority Government without attempting to form a coalition with any other party. Tony Blair had already faced considerable criticism for forcing his Leadership candidate Alun Michael on Welsh Labour; the original choice, Ron Davies, had stepped down after what he described as a 'moment of madness' on Clapham Common. Michael's tenure was to prove short and shaky.

Paddy Ashdown had one further election to fight before stepping down. Euro-elections had never been the happiest of hunting grounds for the Liberal Democrats. The party tended to perform below its standing in the polls. Ashdown had fought hard to establish the fact that the party, while firmly pro-European, was also firmly in favour of reforming the EU. In 1998 he called for a Constitution for Europe to define and limit the powers of Brussels. Under his leadership, the Liberal Democrats had also been the first party to call for a referendum on the euro.

The 1999 Euro-campaign was subsequently criticised in the party for not concentrating sufficiently on European issues. The truth was that it was very difficult to get the media to concentrate on the campaign at all. It took place only just over a month after the local, Scottish and Welsh elections. There was a great deal of election fatigue amongst media, voters and activists alike.

Nonetheless, there were two major advances on the previous Euro-elections. First, this was a PR election, albeit on a regional-list system which was not the party's ideal. Ten Liberal Democrats were elected, compared with the three who had been in the previous European Parliament. Since the MEPs were elected for whole regions, this meant that the Liberal Democrats had an MEP in every region of the country, except for the North East and Wales. As a result, it helped subsequently to give the party a voice in areas like the East Midlands where it had previously had very little presence.

The second advance was in the system of selection. The party in England had devised a scheme known as 'zipping'. Members in each region were asked to elect separately a list of women and a list of men. It had been decided that the regions would be split evenly into those with a man at the top of the list and those led by a woman. Then the lists were zipped together, so that if a woman was first, a man was second, a woman third and so on. Of the ten MEPs elected, five were men and five were women. Among those taking their seats in Brussels were Liz Lynne, the former MP for Rochdale, and Emma Nicholson, the former Conservative MP who was now on the Liberal Democrat benches in the House of Lords.

By announcing his departure so far in advance, Paddy Ashdown guaranteed himself more farewell appearances than the legendary Dame Nellie Melba did. There was his last conference speech in March; his last rally, for the European elections in the Playhouse Theatre; his last party political broadcast, where he talked about the fairer and more caring society for which he had fought and the importance of peace and prosperity in Europe; and numerous farewell dinners and parties. They were all emotional occasions, not least for Paddy Ashdown himself. Even those in the party who had had strong disagreements with him recognised the contribution which he had made. He had ensured survival, and had then secured a series of very significant breakthroughs. He had also played a significant role on the national stage, notably in championing the rights of the Hong Kong Chinese and the Bosnian Muslims.

There was still a long way to go. The media had often levied the one-man-band charge at the Liberal Democrats. Now that one man was packing up his instruments. The future was in the melting pot once again.

8 Effective Opposition, 1999–2003

The Ashdown succession race was not supposed to begin until the Euro-elections were over, but with almost six months' notice of the starting gun it was not surprising that feet crept across the line from time to time. There were no fewer than nine possible contenders, although only five names remained after nominations had closed.

The supposition had been that the field would consist of a pro-Project candidate, an anti-Project candidate and the favourite Charles Kennedy, who was seen as a candidate for unity. In the event, none of the potential pro-Project candidates made it to the starting gate. Menzies Campbell was a highly effective performer on the media and in Parliament. He was a former Olympic athlete, and when it became known that there would be an election, claimed that he thought he could still beat any of his colleagues at 'the hundred yard dash'. The one disadvantage which he suffered was his age. He was an almost exact contemporary of Paddy Ashdown.

Campbell and Kennedy had made a deal. If Paddy Ashdown had decided to step down early in the Parliament, Campbell would put his name forward. If he stepped down late in the Parliament, the contender would be Kennedy. The terms of the deal did not provide for the circumstances which actually arose, with Ashdown announcing his retirement to coincide almost precisely with the mid-point of the Parliament. Campbell, whose parliamentary responsibilities had been more onerous than Kennedy's, believed that Kennedy had prepared the ground for a leadership contest much better than he had. He was doubtful about his chances, conscious of the sacrifices which the Leadership entailed and, being an almost exact contemporary of Ashdown, aware that the party members might want to give the next generation a chance. In the end, he did not put his name forward.

Nick Harvey was another possible contender. He had chaired the Campaigns and Communications Committee, and was highly rated by Paddy Ashdown, who had promoted his career so as to present the party with a choice. Harvey's problem was lack of national profile. Aged only thirty-seven, he felt that he could bide his time. The third pro-Project possible was Don Foster, the MP for Bath who had been Education spokesman. Foster mounted a campaign backed by two high-flying members of the 1997 intake, Mark Oaten and Lembit Opik. They produced leaflets and even T-shirts, which are now something of a collector's item. Foster took part in some of the early hustings meetings. But then he too decided to withdraw, in the belief that he did not have enough support.

Briefly, it seemed as if the Chief Whip Paul Tyler might enter the lists. However, after seeking reassurances from Charles Kennedy, four leading figures from the Ashdown inner circle – Tyler, Harvey, Campbell and Archy Kirkwood –announced that they would be supporting him.

That left four contenders who were more sceptical about The Project: Simon Hughes, Malcolm Bruce, David Rendel and Jackie Ballard. Jackie Ballard had only been in the House since 1997, but decided that it was wrong that this should be an all-male race. She launched her campaign with a helicopter trip and an eye-catching 'Jackie B' logo.

The party had decreed an exhausting round of hustings meetings with a final declaration of the result on 9 August. Charles Kennedy was the best known of the five. He had been President of the party, and had a high media profile which stretched to chat and comedy shows like *Have I Got News for You* as well as news and current affairs programmes. Simon Hughes was judged to have won many of the hustings meetings. In revivalist preacher mode, he made a striking contrast with Kennedy's more laid-back approach. None of the other three candidates stood much serious chance of winning. After the votes of the lower-placed contenders had been redistributed, Kennedy was left with 28,425 against 21,833 for Hughes.

The result was announced in the basement of the Commonwealth Club on Northumberland Avenue. The intention was to find somewhere which looked modern, to underline the fact that this was a party of the future. The disadvantage was that the space available proved distinctly cramped for the purpose, and that it became extremely hot. However, the party proved to the broadcasters that it was capable of split-second timing. The event was carried live by the BBC, and gave the Liberal Democrats some useful profile.

Charles Kennedy recapitulated the themes which he had emphasised during his campaign in his acceptance speech:

> *I pledge to stand up for social justice. To speak up for the disadvantaged whose voices aren't heard by New Labour. To reconnect with the people who feel that political parties offer no solution to the problems that they face. To fight also to improve the public services – the schools and hospitals – on which everyone in Britain depends. This means engaging seriously with the electorate on the core social justice issue: how to pay for decent public services. We have a duty to fight for a clean, safe environment and a better quality of life.*

Simon Hughes had come an unexpectedly good second, and was moved by Charles Kennedy from the Health portfolio to Home Affairs.

Malcolm Bruce had also done better than anticipated. He had been Treasury spokesman. With the help of David Laws, who acted as both his researcher and Director of Policy for the party, he had exposed some embarrassing double-counting in Gordon Brown's economic figures. Revelations about the black hole and the war chest had done much to boost the party's profile. Now Bruce moved to a new role as Chair of the Parliamentary Party.

The senior positions under Paddy Ashdown had all been filled by MPs who had been in the House before 1997. Under Charles Kennedy, the new intake achieved greater prominence. Phil Willis took on the Education portfolio, Steve Webb was promoted to lead on Social Security and Vince Cable became Trade and Industry spokesman. The senior MPs had already been meeting weekly, styled as team leaders. Now it was decided to call them the 'Liberal Democrat Shadow Cabinet'. The party's press releases started referring to spokespeople as 'Shadow Secretary of State' for whatever their portfolio was. The media began increasingly to accept the description. It was just one more sign of the party raising its game, and being seen to compete on an equal footing with the Conservatives and Labour.

The change from Ashdown to Kennedy was more a switch of style than of substance. The meetings at eight in the morning which had been a regular feature during Ashdown's leadership ceased immediately. Kennedy's approach was more relaxed and more consensual. He was less likely than his predecessor to put himself a hundred yards in front of his troops and shout 'follow me'.

There was a clear generational change. When Paddy Ashdown stepped down, he was fifty-eight. Charles Kennedy was thirty-nine. He was seven years younger than the Prime Minister, though a little over a year older than William Hague. It meant that all three parties were now led by relatively young men. Asked about the kind of relationship which he was likely to establish with Tony Blair, Kennedy said he thought that his musical tastes were closer to the Prime Minister's than Ashdown's had been.

There was one early indication of the change which this age difference made. In one of his first interviews after becoming Leader, Charles Kennedy was asked by Andy McSmith of the *Observer* about his attitude to drugs. He said that he was in favour of a Royal Commission on the issue. This was no more than party policy, but it gave the *Observer* its headline. McSmith wrote that Kennedy had stepped into a political minefield. When the party conference had adopted the policy a few years earlier, it had been against Paddy Ashdown's advice and he had walked off the platform. Kennedy had sensed that the public mood on drugs was changing fast. His judgement was vindicated when at the Conservative conference later in the year, Ann Widdecombe championed a tough policy on cannabis, only to discover seven members of the Conservative front bench confessing to having experimented with it.

As a self-confessed disciple of Roy Jenkins and a former Europe spokesman for the party, Charles Kennedy set great store by the European cause. On the fringe of his first autumn conference as Leader in Harrogate, he spoke at an inaugural meeting of the Britain in Europe campaign. Echoing the experience of the referendum campaign of 1975 which had been so important in the political development of his mentor Roy Jenkins, Kennedy said, 'Britain in Europe is a test-bed for the new politics we want to create. I have always said we should co-operate with sensible Conservatives as well as pro-European Labour people on issues where we agree. Now we have to operate to translate our convictions into action.'

In October 1999, Kennedy appeared on the platform at the official inauguration of Britain in Europe, alongside Tony Blair, Gordon Brown, Robin Cook, Michael Heseltine and Kenneth Clarke. As the prospects for a referendum on the Jenkins Report receded, he fought hard for a referendum on the euro and became increasingly critical of the

Government's failure to give a lead on the issue. The Liberal Democrats were later to establish their own commission of expert economists to assess whether Gordon Brown's five tests on the euro had been met; they reported that this was indeed the case.

The party became increasingly frustrated by Labour's over-caution on the euro. However, the Liberal Democrat stance did help to encourage more pro-European Tories to change allegiance. Bill Newton-Dunn was a sitting Euro-MP and a former leader of the Conservative group. His defection brought the party's strength in Brussels up to eleven, and gave the Liberal Democrats another useful parliamentary presence in the East Midlands, previously something of a black hole. Then in the early stages of the general election campaign, the former MP John Lee announced that he was joining the party, the first Tory ex-minister to do so.

Compared with previous Parliaments, there were far fewer parliamentary by-elections after 1997. This was a cause of frustration to the Liberal Democrats, who had always benefited nationally from the attention which a by-election win could bring them. Charles Kennedy's first taste of electoral success was in a council by-election. The party was one seat short of controlling the London Borough of Islington. It was a substantial prize to capture, both as the home of Tony Blair until he moved to Downing Street, and as a notorious bastion of the loony left in the 1980s. When a vacancy arose in a hitherto safe Labour seat, the party threw enormous effort into the contest and the Liberal Democrat candidate Paul Fox stormed home.

Then in February 2000, the Tory MP for Romsey, Michael Colvin, died in tragic circumstances in a fire at his home. When the Liberal Democrats had taken seats off the Conservatives in the 1990s, it had been in a period when the Tories were in power and highly unpopular. Winning a very safe seat from the Conservatives when they were in opposition was a much taller order. Nonetheless, the Rennard machine swung into action. The candidate was Sandra Gidley, a local pharmacist who had been Mayor of the town. The Conservatives, as they had done so often, picked the wrong man. Tim Palmer was an old-Etonian farmer who came from Dorset, a point which the Liberal Democrat leaflets never failed to point out.

The Conservatives appeared to misunderstand the nature of the constituency. They fought the election as if Romsey was largely rural and agricultural. In fact, boundary changes had meant that a very significant section of it was suburban; it took in Chandler's Ford and other substantial sections of the suburbs of Southampton. These areas were very receptive to the Liberal Democrat message. Many of the voters had converted to Labour in the Blair euphoria of 1997, and could be persuaded by persistent canvassing to switch either tactically or out of conviction to the Liberal Democrats. The miserly 75p increase in the pension at the previous Budget was a powerful incentive to convince them to change allegiance. Another advantage was that Romsey adjoined two constituencies already held by Liberal Democrats: Winchester and Eastleigh. This meant that the party had a higher profile in the local media and it was easier to convince voters that it stood a real chance of winning.

During the Romsey campaign, the Conservative leader William Hague was taking a high-profile right-wing stance on both asylum and law and order. He attacked the verdict against the Norfolk farmer Tony Martin, who had shot a burglar. Despite the misgivings of some Liberal Democrat campaigners, Charles Kennedy hit back hard against Hague on both issues. It was argued that standing up for Liberal values might harm the party when it was trying to fight a traditional Conservative bastion. But Romsey was won convincingly. The majority was 3,311 on a 12.6% swing from Conservatives to Liberal Democrats. Labour lost their deposit. Charles Kennedy, who had paid numerous visits to the constituency, called the result 'a triumph for the politics of hope over the politics of fear'.

The result undermined any advantage to the Conservatives from the modest local council gains which they achieved the same night. The Liberal Democrats could argue that a by-election, in which there was a much higher turnout, was a stronger test of public opinion than council elections. In any case, the party had put in a very strong performance at the council elections as well, with 28%, compared with 29% for Labour and 37% for the Conservatives. Oldham and Cambridge were added to the tally of councils under Liberal Democrat control. Labour, meanwhile, had suffered the setback of Ken Livingstone's victory in the elections for Mayor of London.

So the Liberal Democrats had the most reason for satisfaction from the results, a conclusion endorsed by Hugo Young in the *Guardian*. He wrote that the Romsey result 'signalled the deep illness if not the death of Tory England'. As for Charles Kennedy, he suggested that he was a new kind of politician who was suited to a new era. 'He's absolved from hate,' Young wrote. 'In an age when people have many fewer expectations of politicians, demanding mainly that they don't agitate the voters' cynicism, Kennedy's inoffensiveness, his obscurity, his conversational style when he's heard at all, are more than a timely asset. They may signal a politics that's out of others' reach.' The Liberal Democrats would not entirely accept Young's description of their Leader, but he had identified an asset which was to become increasingly obvious as time went on. Charles Kennedy had won the Leadership promising to tackle the problem that ordinary people do not connect with politics; now he was proving that he had ways of connecting with them himself that other politicians were lacking.

Romsey also proved that the mistakes of the Conservative Government were still fresh in people's minds, a factor which augured well for the next general election. At the autumn conference in Bournemouth in 2000, the Liberal Democrats spelt out how they planned to position themselves for the forthcoming general election:

there was to be no return to equidistance. Relations with the Labour Government might have cooled, but whereas Labour had been a great disappointment, a return to the Conservatives would be a disaster.

Meanwhile, the Liberal Democrats had joined the Government in Wales. When Alun Michael's minority Labour administration faced a vote of confidence, Tony Blair had pleaded with Charles Kennedy to persuade the Welsh Liberal Democrats to support Michael. Kennedy was no more prepared to lean on the Welsh party than Ashdown had been to tell the Scottish Party what to do the previous year. He pointed out to the Prime Minister that he believed in devolution. What Liberal Democrat members of the Welsh Assembly did was entirely a matter for them. Alun Michael duly stepped down in advance of his inevitable defeat.

His successor as Welsh Labour Leader was Rhodri Morgan, who immediately began talks with the Liberal Democrats. Michael German and his colleagues were in a strong position; it would have been very difficult for Labour to continue as a minority administration. The Welsh Liberal Democrats persuaded Morgan to include more or less the whole of their manifesto from the previous year in the Government's programme. At first, there were strong misgivings amongst Welsh Liberal Democrat activists. But after intensive consultation and a special conference at Builth Wells, the partnership was endorsed and Michael German and Jenny Randerson became ministers.

As the UK general election of 2001 approached, the media tended to be dismissive of Liberal Democrat prospects. Their assumption was that 1997 had been a bit of a freak. The forty-six seat tally was highly unlikely to be repeated. Tory recovery might be too modest to unseat the Labour Government, but it was bound to push the Liberal Democrats back. The veteran MORI pollster Robert Worcester predicted that there would be thirty-two Liberal Democrat MPs in the next Parliament. There were good odds to be had at the bookmakers on an increase in Liberal Democrat seats.

The party had long set itself that target. Tim Razzall, who chaired the campaign, and Chris Rennard, now established beyond doubt as the wiliest and most experienced campaign strategist in British politics, were convinced that the party could not only win more seats than in 1997 but also a higher proportion of the vote. The second objective was probably harder than the first; despite the success in 1997, the party's percentage share had actually dropped at every election since 1983.

In 2001, the Liberal Democrats were able to mount a more professional campaign than ever before. Their full-time press and policy teams were far more substantial than they had been in the past. Outside volunteers came in to provide invaluable support on, for instance, the night team, but the core staff had been used to working together for many months. Continuity was an important bonus. Meanwhile, the well-regarded independent production company Tiger Aspect was working on the party election broadcasts, and the advertising consultancy Banc were advising on posters and messaging. After much research and soul searching, Banc came up with the slogan 'a real chance for a real change'.

The line which really caught on, however, was that 'you can't get something for nothing'. There was still widespread dissatisfaction with the public services. Labour was ruling out raising income tax, and the Conservatives were talking about tax and expenditure cuts. The Liberal Democrats once again gained both credibility and distinctiveness by advocating a penny on income tax for education. There was also to be a 50p-in-the-pound higher rate of income tax on incomes above £100,000, which was to be used for the health service and for improved pensions. As at the previous election, the Institute for Fiscal Studies acknowledged that the Liberal Democrats' sums added up. The BBC economics correspondent Evan Davies said the same thing.

One break with the past for 2001 was the style of the manifesto. 'Freedom, Justice, Honesty' was published in the form of a tabloid newspaper. A further innovation was the presence in each chapter of a green box, explaining how there was an environmental dimension to each of the policy areas. Friends of the Earth were to give the Liberal Democrats a higher environmental rating than either Labour or the Conservatives and equal to that of the Greens. It was a source of frustration during the campaign that the media paid so little attention to the environmental agenda. In an interview on *Newsnight*, Kirsty Wark suggested to Charles Kennedy that there was little of substance separating Liberal Democrat and Labour policies. He retorted that there was the environment for a start. 'Maybe very marginal issues like the environment,' said Wark. Kennedy snapped back, 'You call the future of the planet a marginal issue?'

A further objective of the campaign was 'to promote Charles Kennedy as a successful, capable strong leader who understands people's concerns and puts forward honest and sensible proposals to address them'. Kennedy's personal poll ratings were good, although at the start of the election campaign he was not as well known as Blair or Hague. Nevertheless, in the Liberal Democrat camp, nobody could be sure how he would perform under the stresses and strains of a general election campaign.

In the event, Charles Kennedy confounded his critics and had an exceptionally good election. He could claim great personal credit for the result. Some had doubted his stamina, but under the enormous pressure of the campaign he proved to possess substantial reserves of it. His programme involved visiting three regional media centres a day. The theory was that there was more airtime and impact available to the Liberal Democrats on the regional media than on the national stage, so that this was the best way to maximise the effectiveness of the Leader, but it made for an exhausting schedule. In addition to this, Kennedy attended nearly all the national press conferences, did a series of major national media interviews and spoke at five rallies. It was impressive by any standards.

Mistakes by the other parties certainly helped to improve the Liberal Democrats' standing during the campaign, and Kennedy was able to make the most of the breaks that he was given. It was clear from the outset that the Conservatives were not going to make any serious attempt to move onto the centre ground. Their strategy appeared to be to hold onto their core vote as far as possible and hope that it turned out in greater numbers than the rest.

In the run-up to the election, at the Conservative Spring Forum in Harrogate, William Hague made his notorious 'foreign land' speech. Although he began with the line 'let me take you on a journey to a foreign land', he denied that it was intended to be xenophobic. The tone nonetheless implied that he believed the country was being overrun by foreigners. 'Talk about Europe', he said, 'and they call you extreme. Talk about tax and they call you greedy. Talk about crime and they call you reactionary. Talk about asylum and they call you a racist. Talk about your nation and they call you Little Englanders.'

The Labour Party, no doubt guided by their focus groups, were muted in their reaction. By far the strongest response came from Charles Kennedy in a speech on 14 March. 'By his use of emotive language over the issue of asylum and immigration,' he said, 'and now by his claim that Britain is becoming "a foreign land", William is playing on some people's fears and pandering to some people's prejudices. William Hague is not a racist – but by choosing his language so carelessly, he shows himself to be soft on racism and soft on the causes of racism.'

Labour's campaign did not go particularly smoothly either. Tony Blair made the mistake of announcing the election in a school at a religious assembly full of children who were too young to vote. It looked as if the spin and control-freakery had gone too far, a danger to which the Liberal Democrats had often drawn attention. Then he was berated over the state of the health service in Birmingham by Sharon Storer, one of the rare ordinary members of the public who managed to get access to him.

Again, this played straight to the Liberal Democrat message that Labour had been very disappointing in not investing properly in health and education. The same day saw the most memorable event of the election campaign – the rumble in Rhyl, when John Prescott got into a fight with a protester.

The election took place against the backdrop of the foot and mouth outbreak, which had caused much of the countryside to be closed off. In one sense, this was unhelpful to the Liberal Democrats. The Tories made more of the running on the issue. It may in fact have helped the Conservatives to save one or two rural seats like Westmorland and Lonsdale. The Liberal Democrats were too slow to come out in favour of postponing the election, which opened them up to the charge of fence-sitting. On the other hand, in many constituencies, the postponement allowed the Liberal Democrats more time to build support. It also gave the headquarters team a brief opportunity to recharge batteries.

A major aim of the Liberal Democrat campaign was to build on the appeal of Charles Kennedy. The first party election broadcast was a profile of the Leader, a successor to Hugh Hudson's 'Kinnock – the Movie' and the 'Ashdown – the Movie' broadcast of 1997. Charles Kennedy has the advantage of living in one of the most beautiful parts of Scotland. The croft just outside Fort William which he inherited from his grandfather stands next to his parents' croft. Both have spectacular views of Ben Nevis. The area made an outstanding backdrop to the film.

Ian and Mary Kennedy also made very good television subjects. Among other accomplishments, they were both musicians, Ian on the fiddle and Mary on the piano. They were also unspinnable. Lesley White, the *Sunday Times* journalist, was in Fort William at the same time as the broadcast was being filmed, writing a major profile of Charles for the *Sunday Times Magazine*. Mary Kennedy confided in her that she feared that the Liberal Democrats were set to lose seats. She just hoped that Charles held his so that he still had a job.

Some of the footage from 'Kennedy – the Movie' inevitably ended up on the cutting room floor. Kennedy was filmed playing golf with his old schoolteacher Bob Dick. The difficulty was that filming took place in February, and much of the golf course was covered in snow. Kennedy managed to hit some shots on one of the few green patches of the course, and cutaways were duly filmed of an increasingly frozen Bob Dick calling out 'Good shot, Charles'. The footage actually shown was much truer to life.

There was one extremely alarming day during the campaign. The turboprop which was transporting the Leader's tour up to the Midlands hit an air pocket. The luggage fell down from the ceiling. There were cuts and bruises, and for a brief period those on board thought that their ends were nigh. As Euan Ferguson wrote the following weekend in the *Observer*, 'The Special Branch bodyguard watching from the runway told them later, quietly, that he thought it was "all over". Kaput and finito; a nasty little crash, and the end of the third party in British politics.'

That was only the first of the vicissitudes of that day. The route from Birmingham Airport to Ludlow and back featured an epic traffic jam. The tour began to run seriously behind time. The next stop had to be cancelled. Instead of flying to Sussex to visit Lewes, Charles Kennedy went straight to Newcastle to take part in a special edition of *Question Time* with David Dimbleby. The team which had driven down to Sussex to brief him during the flight instead flew on their own up to Newcastle for a hurried session in a hotel.

Yet somehow, after all this, Kennedy managed to put in a commanding performance on *Question Time* in which he had the audience eating out of his hand. This was a turning point of the campaign. After *Question Time*, the Liberal Democrats knew that they had a huge asset in their Leader. Kennedy's personal popularity ran ahead of both Blair's and Hague's in the polls, and the ratings for the party itself started a steady climb.

As the campaign drew towards its close, the Liberal Democrats began to introduce a new theme. It was clear by this stage that the Conservatives were making little impact and were heading for another disastrous result. Charles Kennedy started to talk about his party as 'the effective opposition'. The term did not entail a prediction that the party would actually overhaul the Conservatives in numbers of seats. It simply meant that the Liberal Democrats' criticisms of the Government had far more force than those made by the Conservatives. This applied in particular to public services, where a party pledged to cut taxes was bound to be unconvincing in any plan which it put forward to improve schools and hospitals.

The final Liberal Democrat rally took place in west London. With the veteran film critic Barry Norman in the chair, Charles Kennedy expressed his satisfaction that the other parties had started to echo his catchphrase 'you can't get something for nothing'. He stressed the effective-opposition theme strongly, and then pushed home a powerful message which had been developed by Chris Rennard:

> *If you think that the Government has done enough over the past four years for the NHS, education and pensioners, then you should vote Labour. If you think that the Government should do even less to fund public services and pensions, and support their irresponsible tax cuts, then you should vote Conservative. But if you think there should be more investment in the NHS and education and that we need to do more for pensioners, then you can only vote Liberal Democrat.*

Strong though those words were, they were somewhat upstaged by the appearance at the rally of a streaker. The Liberal Democrats had always prided themselves on the fact that, unlike the all-ticket occasions staged by Labour and the Conservatives, their rallies were open to anybody. It was also notable that the party's stewards were considerably faster at catching the streaker than the Special Branch men looking after Charles Kennedy. Kennedy wondered out loud whether it was more appropriate to quote Harry Truman's line that if you can't stand the heat, get out of the kitchen, or Nye Bevan's words about not going naked into the conference chamber.

When the party's headquarters staff gathered at the London restaurant Pizza on the Park to watch the results, they were confident that it would be a good night. Overall, the Liberal Democrats ended up with fifty-two seats, six more than they had had after 1997. The pundits' predictions that they would fall back had been confounded. Among the most spectacular results were the victories in previously 'true blue' Guildford and in Tony Benn's old Labour heartland of Chesterfield. This time, all seven of the retiring MPs managed to hand their seats on to a Liberal Democrat successor. David Laws, the economist whose research had made such an impact in the previous Parliament, became the new MP for Paddy Ashdown's old seat of Yeovil. John Thurso succeeded Robert Maclennan in Caithness and Sutherland, becoming the first hereditary peer to move from the Lords to the Commons. Furthermore, the percentage share of the vote was up on 1997 by 1.6%. And in Scotland, the Liberal Democrats had driven the Conservatives into fourth place in the national share of the vote.

2001 proved to have been one of the most successful of the campaigns which the party and its predecessors had fought. The percentage share of the vote rose from 13% to nearly 19% during the course of the election. Asked by MORI which of the parties had impressed most during the campaign, 11% said the Conservatives, 20% the Labour Party and 30% the Liberal Democrats.

There were two casualties. Jackie Ballard lost by the narrowest of margins in Taunton. She had been a strong campaigner against hunting in a seat where the pursuit had some zealous adherents. She also undoubtedly suffered from the foot and mouth crisis. She was eventually to be appointed to head the RSPCA. The other loser was Dr Peter Brand, who was ousted in the Isle of Wight, a constituency whose island ways are often at odds with trends on the mainland.

Once again, there was a shortage of women in the new parliamentary party. The final tally was five. The twenty-seven-year-old Jenny Willott was close to winning in Cardiff Central. Had she and Jackie Ballard been returned, the total would have looked a bit better, but the party still had some way to go on the issue of gender balance.

Post-election prospects looked good for the Liberal Democrats. It was clear now that 1997 had not just been a flash in the pan. There had been a pattern of steady expansion and growth which could be traced right back to 1990 and the Eastbourne by-election. Similarly, the Conservative Party was flatlining as it had done for the past nine years. In the Conservative Leadership election of 2001, the party rejected the two candidates, Kenneth Clarke and Michael Portillo, who might have led them back towards the centre ground, in favour of Iain Duncan Smith, who appeared to offer no more than reassurance to the faithful.

Meanwhile, the Labour Government had been given the benefit of the doubt in 2001, but the shine was coming off, and the chances were that it would come off further as the new Parliament progressed. This was not yet the big breakthrough, but the opportunities for the Liberal Democrats were looking better than they had done since the early 1980s.

The first half of the new Parliament was dominated by international issues. The tragedy of September 11th 2001 took place only days before the Liberal Democrat conference. Charles Kennedy had spent most of his brief period of pre-parliamentary adult life in Indiana as a Fulbright Scholar. He spoke with heartfelt sympathy for the American people. When the issue of overthrowing the Taleban in Afghanistan arose, there were anxieties in the party, but Kennedy and Menzies Campbell rallied the MPs behind the allied effort, while voicing their opposition to the use of cluster bombs and making it clear that they did not want to see the pursuit of Al Qaeda extended to an attack on Iraq or any other country. Kennedy said that the Liberal Democrats would give the Government no blank cheques, and that the Government in its turn should give the Americans no blank cheques. They should stand shoulder to shoulder with the Americans, but be prepared to give them a tap on the shoulder when necessary.

When the US Government then duly did decide to attack Iraq, the Liberal Democrats quickly voiced their reservations. Their position was a delicate one. Charles Kennedy had come into politics as a member of the SDP. He was no friend of the Labour left. He deplored their knee-jerk anti-Americanism and their assumption that there was a capitalist conspiracy to dominate the world. On the other hand, he subscribed wholeheartedly to the party's internationalist outlook, and its deep commitment to the United Nations. The party strongly agreed that the UN must take the lead, and in particular, where there was a question whether Saddam Hussein possessed weapons of mass destruction, that was up to Hans Blix and the UN inspectors to determine.

As the United States administration came closer and closer to using force, dragging an apparently impotent British Government in its wake, the Liberal Democrats were lining up firmly with the opponents of the war. There was an honourable precedent in Jo Grimond's opposition to the Suez adventure.

In the Commons, the Liberal Democrat stance on Iraq justified the claim that they and not the Conservatives were the effective opposition. The Conservatives, who had strong links with the right of the Republican Party, gave the Government uncritical support. The Liberal Democrats were the only party questioning Tony Blair's policy. When the Conservatives started heckling Charles Kennedy for questioning

Tony Blair at excessive length, he turned round to them and retorted, 'I am asking the questions which the honourable members on those benches have failed to ask.' The taunt hit home.

On 15 February 2003, Charles Kennedy took part in the demonstration against the war in London's Hyde Park, the largest such gathering in British history. It was a risky strategy – party leaders do not usually take to the streets in demonstrations. Some of the other participants, like Tony Benn, Tariq Ali and George Galloway, were not natural allies of the Liberal Democrats.

The predominant slogan on the march was 'Not in my name', but the Liberal Democrats marched under a banner which read 'Give peace a chance'. Their position was that war against Saddam could not be ruled out, but that it should only take place with the agreement of the United Nations and after the weapons inspectors had decided that their mission could get no further. Kennedy told the rally, 'I'm not persuaded of the case for war. The arguments have been contradictory and inconsistent and the information has all too often been misleading as well as inconclusive … If the great powers of the world ignore the United Nations, then great damage will be done to world order and to the best hope for international justice in the world.'

Tony Blair did concede one of the preconditions on which the Liberal Democrats had insisted before being prepared to back military action. He allowed a debate and a vote in the House of Commons. While the other parties were split, all fifty-three Liberal Democrat MPs went into the same lobby against the Government. The Foreign Secretary Jack Straw joked about 'the iron discipline of the Liberal Democrats'. It was a description which nobody could have used about the party or its predecessors in previous years, even in jest.

Once the fighting started, the Liberal Democrats were bound to support the British troops – the logical alternative would have been to support Saddam. Spokespeople talked about their desire for a speedy and successful end to the fighting with the minimum of casualties either amongst British troops or amongst Iraqi civilians. The party endured taunts from its opponents of doing a U-turn on the war, but there was no contradiction between opposing the war and backing the troops, and the Liberal Democrat position was mirrored by other opponents of the war like the former Labour Cabinet ministers Robin Cook and Chris Smith, and former Tory ministers like Kenneth Clarke. Meanwhile, the party switched its attention to the aftermath of the war, calling for the full involvement of the United Nations in reconstruction.

There was a slight downturn in the Liberal Democrats' poll rating after the war, but as events in the Middle East continue to unfold, the stance which the party has taken is looking to being increasingly vindicated. Above all, the party had called for the UN weapons inspectors to be given time to complete their work. With no sign of the weapons of mass destruction in the aftermath of the war, that position is looking increasingly to be vindicated.

There have been important developments on the domestic front since the 2001 election. The party's leaders recognised that the time had come to revise the policies which had stood the Liberal Democrats in good stead for the past three general elections. The party had never believed in high taxation for its own sake. It did not want to be in a position where whatever the Labour Government was planning to spend, the Liberal Democrats would say they would spend more. Having stuck to Tory spending plans during the early years, the Blair Government was belatedly planning to invest more. In his 2002 Budget, Gordon Brown announced a rise in National Insurance which would raise considerable extra funds for schools and hospitals. Since the new money available was equivalent to the extra resources which the Liberal Democrats had promised in their 2001 Manifesto, it made no sense to try and outbid the Government. The penny on income tax appeared to have served its purpose.

For the long term, the party set up a commission on public services headed by the MEP and economist Chris Huhne. Its conclusions were agreed at the 2002 party conference. It advocated replacing National Insurance with an NHS contribution earmarked for the Health Service. That way, Huhne argued, there would be guaranteed funding for health for the long-term future; the health budget would no longer depend on a tap turned up or down by the Chancellor every year. The report also proposed extensive devolution of public services, and for a provision for local communities to form mutual organisations to take over the running of hospitals and schools.

The Huhne message chimed in with regular attacks on the Government for overcentralisation, bureaucracy and setting targets which distort priorities in health and education. The Conservatives were also trying to score points on these issues, but their credibility was fatally damaged both by their record in office and by their stated aim to reduce public spending.

The Liberal Democrats continued to attract previous supporters of other parties. In December 2001, the Labour MP for Shrewsbury and Atcham Paul Marsden crossed the floor of the House of Commons to become the fifty-third Liberal Democrat member. He complained that the Government was intolerant of dissent and that he had been bullied by the Labour whips. By an accident of timing, the Pro-Euro Conservative Party joined the Liberal Democrats en bloc the same day. They included two former Conservative MEPs, John Stevens and Brendan Donnelly, together with another former MP, Sir Anthony Meyer. In due course, they helped to form the Peel Group, under the chairmanship of Mark Oaten. Its purpose was to encourage other disaffected Conservatives to jump ship and to offer the Liberal Democrats campaigning expertise in opposing Tory candidates.

The mid-term elections in 2003 saw a further advance. The Liberal Democrats took a record 30% of the vote in the council elections. While the Conservatives had 35%, this was a poorer mid-term tally than William Hague had achieved during the previous Parliament. In the Scottish elections, the Liberal Democrats held steady with seventeen seats. With the Greens and the Scottish Socialists making significant advances, both the SNP and the Labour Party fell back substantially. The result was that the Scottish Liberal Democrats were able to drive a harder bargain in the partnership negotiations. Labour agreed to the key Liberal Democrat demand that there should be free eye and dental checks. They also conceded PR for local government. There were to be three Liberal Democrat Cabinet ministers in the Executive instead of two. In Wales too, the Liberal Democrats held on to their existing seats, but here Labour advanced to secure a bare majority, and decided to dispense with the partnership and try to govern on their own.

Now, halfway through the 2001 Parliament, the position of the Liberal Democrats looks encouraging. The Government is faltering. The Conservatives have made only the most modest of recoveries. The Liberal Democrats alone can claim to be making progress. They are substantially ahead of their position in the mid-term of the last Parliament. As always, their fate depends in part on the fortunes of Labour and the Conservatives. If the Conservatives falter, they are well placed to close the gap with them considerably further. If it is Labour which is more obviously faltering, a hung Parliament seems a strong possibility.

But Liberal Democrats have now learnt not to be distracted by speculation about post-election scenarios. They have discovered, particularly from their experience in Scotland, that they need to campaign on their own programme, telling the electors that the more votes they get, the more of that programme will be implemented. Breakthrough is best achieved by not talking about breakthrough.

The party has another advantage, too, compared with the past. There is a new generation of Liberal Democrat candidates and MPs who are determined to win power. Having convinced themselves that the party will be in government in the foreseeable future, they are far better able to go out and convince the electorate.

9   Home Thoughts
from Abroad

British experience so far suggests that the party system is undergoing a slow but steady mutation. It is worth bearing in mind that there is an alternative model, the big bang.

25 October 1993 witnessed one of the most sensational election results ever seen in a western democracy. The Progressive Conservative Party of Canada, founded 126 years earlier, went to the polls as the Government of the country. It had been in power for nine years, and had 169 seats at the dissolution of Parliament. When the votes were counted, the Conservatives had been reduced to precisely two MPs, one in New Brunswick and one in Quebec.

The Conservatives, of course, lost office. That was expected. Periods of Conservative government have been the exception rather than the rule in post-war Canada. In poignant contrast with British experience, the Canadian Liberal Party has been the natural party of government there since 1945, emerging from thirteen out of seventeen general elections with the largest number of seats.

What the Conservatives had failed to anticipate was that they would not even emerge from the election as the main opposition. In fact there were no fewer than three other parties, apart from the victorious

Liberals, which ended up with significantly more seats. The separatist Bloc Québécois became the new official opposition with fifty-four seats. An alternative right-wing party, Reform, based in Alberta and British Columbia, was just behind with fifty-two, whilst the left-wing New Democratic Party had nine members in the new Parliament.

No two countries are alike in any respect, particularly in politics. It is hard to see the British Conservatives falling as far and as fast as their Canadian counterparts. On the eve of poll in 1993, however, John Major believed that Canada and Britain were sufficiently alike that he could phone Kim Campbell and remind her how she could win the election despite the pundits' forecasts, just as he had done in Britain the year before. There are certainly aspects of that famous Canadian election which must still send the occasional chill through the bones of British Tories.

The Progressive Conservative Party in Canada prided themselves on being a truly national party. Their representation was more evenly spread across the country than that of their rivals. That meant that, under the 'first past the post' system which operates in Canada as in Britain, a drop in percentage votes could result in a very disproportionate drop in seats. Despite only holding two constituencies, the Progressive Conservatives won 16% of the vote overall at that 1993 election, only 2.7% behind Reform. They were actually 2.5% ahead of the Bloc Quebecois and 9.1% ahead of the NDP. Their opposition rivals, however, were much better placed to profit from 'first past the post', having strong power bases in particular provinces, whilst being weak or non-existent in others. Meanwhile the Liberals, with a minority 41.3% of the vote, emerged with 60% of the seats.

Another potential parallel lies in one of the key campaign issues. The Progressive Conservative Government had faced an ever-increasing budget deficit over its period in power. In the election campaign, the party pledged to eliminate the deficit within five years. That led the Liberals to allege that the Tories had a secret agenda to cut public spending on social programmes. The Conservative Prime Minister Kim Campbell poured petrol on that particular fire. She promised that her party would 'completely rethink Canada's Social Security', but added that an election campaign was 'not the time to get involved in very, very serious discussions' on the subject. That single statement, which encouraged electors to fear the worst, appears to have lost the Conservatives twelve points in the polls.

There were other factors which may or may not have a bearing on the UK at the time of the next general election. The Progressive Conservatives had changed Leader only months before they went to the polls in October 1993. The move did nothing to help them. Brian Mulroney had achieved the lowest ratings of any Prime Minister in Canadian history. But his successor Kim Campbell, once claimed to combine the talents of Margaret Thatcher and the singer Madonna, was to prove more unpopular still. The style and personality of the leaders proved a key factor in the 1993 Canadian election, and it worked very much to the disadvantage of the Conservatives.

British Tory leaders have had a taste of the kind of press that Mrs Campbell was getting. Writing her political obituary when it was all over, the *Toronto Financial Post*, for instance, said:

> *Of all the leaders running for office this time, she was the one who listened to voters least. Which would have been okay if there had been substance, but there was precious little of that either.*
>
> *Nor was there much style. At a time when a discombobulated country needed personal therapy, Campbell offered political theory. Where Canadians sought out hope, she served up hectoring. When a candidate cannot convey hope, she has at least to offer reassurance. If that's not forthcoming, then there must be policy.*

> *And if the candidate fails those three tests, the only thing*
> *remaining is to tapdance valiantly. Campbell lacked even such a*
> *basic skill as that.*

The Canadian Conservatives fought a campaign of extraordinary ineptness. As they continued to slide in the polls, they became more and more desperate. They drew attention in two television advertisements to the fact that the Liberal Leader Jean Chrétien suffered from facial paralysis. People were shown saying that they would be embarrassed to have a Prime Minister with a deformity. The ads shocked the voters and did the Conservatives enormous further damage. By the time the party decided to withdraw them, it was too late. Academic studies have suggested that without these commercials, the Conservatives could have ended up with as many as sixty seats instead of only two.

The Conservatives were the main losers from the fact that Canadian politics was no longer dominated by two big parties. The results in 1993 showed that the Conservatives lost votes significantly to their rivals on the right in the Reform Party and to the Bloc Québécois, as well as to the Liberals. Conservative rhetoric actually sounded more hostile to Reform, their rivals on the right, than to any of their other opponents.

There is another potential parallel with British politics. Canada has seen a significant rise in the numbers of people disillusioned with politics and distrustful of politicians. At the same time, turnout in elections has steadily dropped. In 1979, according to Gallup, 30% of the population expressed confidence in political parties in Canada. By 1989, the figure was 18%, and by 1994 only 9%. In such circumstances, loyalties to one party or another are very weak.

There has never been a huge ideological divide in Canadian politics. Before 1993, the tradition was alternation between a conservative Liberal Party and a liberal Conservative Party. Over the years, Conservative Governments have supported public enterprises like the railways and the Ontario Hydroelectric Corporation, while the Liberals have found themselves cutting public spending. The strong identification with class politics or with the left or the right, which is weakening so much in Britain, never existed to any great extent in Canada in the first place. All this made it that much easier for their opponents to detach large numbers of voters from the Conservative camp.

The Progressive Conservatives were not wiped out altogether in 1993. Under the Canadian federal system, the provincial legislatures are extremely important, and the Tories retained their power bases there. A decade on, they continue to vie with Reform, now renamed Alliance, for the role of official opposition.

The Canadian experience shows that the greater the number of viable parties there is in a democracy, the more a 'first past the post' system is likely to distort the results. At the same time, however, if disillusionment with traditional parties is sufficiently strong, the electoral system cannot indefinitely stifle the growth of other political forces.

Nonetheless, without 'first past the post', British political parties would have almost certainly fragmented long ago on the kind of lines which may be seen in most countries in the rest of western Europe. On the right-to-left spectrum, we begin with parties of the hard right like the French Front National, the Italian Alleanza Nazionale, the Belgian Vlaams Blok, the Austrian Freedom Party, the Danish People's Party and the Dutch List Fortuyn. Then there are the centre-right parties, which in most countries sail under Christian Democrat colours. Next there are the Liberals, and then the Socialists. Finally, there are the neo- and not-so-neo-Communist parties. It is harder to place on the spectrum the Green and regional parties, some of which also have considerable support.

The British Conservative Party has traditionally been a coalition between natural Christian Democrats and those who would feel quite comfortable in the Front National. When I made a documentary about

Jean-Marie Le Pen in 1991, he repeatedly protested to me that his view of the world was very similar to Margaret Thatcher's.

It is important to distinguish the man from the programme. Le Pen has done things which even the most ferociously right-wing British Conservative would never countenance. He has talked of the gas chambers as a detail of history. He is suspected of responsibility for atrocities during the Algerian War. His attempts to look the French equivalent of a traditional knight of the shires verge on the ridiculous. He was keen to show me how much he loved animals, presenting first his dog, then his cat and finally, as the *pièce de résistance*, his pet rat. Hitler liked animals too.

So there is no precise equivalence between the right of the Conservative Party and the FN. Nobody would accuse the Tory right of the thuggery which is sometimes associated with the Front National. British spokespeople, however reactionary, are also, for the most part, far more restrained in their use of language; Britain, in my experience, is a significantly less racist country than France.

Nonetheless, the issues which are championed most vociferously by the Conservative right do echo the programme of the FN to a considerable extent. They talk about patriotism, the need to curb immigration and asylum. They call for draconian penalties for criminals and reducing the interference of the European Union. They would be comfortable with the slogan of Vichy France, 'Travail, Famille, Patrie' (Work, Family, Country), with which Le Pen's hero Marshal Pétain replaced the revolutionary motto of 'liberté, égalité, fraternité'.

Until now, all British Conservative leaders since the war would have fitted far more comfortably into the Christian Democrat tradition. That has become, however, very much a minority voice in the Conservative Party. The Tory Party is currently said to be divided between the Doc Martens and the Russell and Bromley tendencies, but even the so-called modernisers would plant their feet firmly on the FN side of the

European argument, against the Christian Democrat position. The grass-roots membership of the Tory Party has always pulled towards the harder right. As numbers shrink, that tendency becomes more pronounced, and the leadership less and less able to resist it, even if it really wanted to do so.

There has been much alarm about the rise of the hard right in continental Europe. There is certainly no room for complacency. However, it is worth noting the limits of the achievements of even the most successful of the hard-line parties. When Jean-Marie Le Pen sent shock waves through Europe by beating the Socialists in May 2002, his vote increased by less than 1% from the previous presidential election. He had 16.86% in the first round, and the reason that he came second instead of the Socialist candidate Lionel Jospin was that the left-wing vote was fragmented between so many candidates. In the second round run-off against Jacques Chirac, Le Pen was only able to increase his score to 17.79%, against 82.21% for Chirac.

The only far-right continental party to have rivalled Le Pen is the Freedom Party in Austria. Jörg Haider did poll nearly 27% in 1999, but in the 2002 election, his party was down to barely 10%, and does not look like recovering. While Haider's party struggled through two and a half years as the junior partner in Government, Pim Fortuyn's list in Holland was in power for only ten months before collapsing almost totally. Fortuyn's high watermark was the 17% scored in the 2002 Dutch general election, a figure inflated by a sympathy vote after Fortuyn himself was assassinated by an animal rights activist shortly before polling day. Amongst other significant continental parties of the hard right, the Danish People's Party won 12% in 2001 while the Flemish Vlaams Bloc emerged from the Belgian general election in 1999 with 9.9%.

Caution is essential in extrapolating from one political tradition to another. But the proportional continental systems do suggest one lesson for British politics. Where voters are given a free option to choose the hard right, it is very unlikely that more than one in five will do so. Therefore, the closer the Conservative Party moves towards embracing a hard-right programme, the more likely it is that its support will shrink. Put another way, the bedrock vote for the hard right in any European country is unlikely to represent much more than 15%.

The jury is out on the British Conservative Party. It blows hot and cold. Sometimes it seems to be moving back towards the centre ground; at other times, it is tempted away. If it were to near that bedrock vote, the consequences under a 'first past the post' system like Britain's would be devastating. It is highly unlikely that the Canadian meltdown scenario would be repeated here, but it is not absolutely impossible. The British Conservatives have already been almost entirely wiped out in Scotland, Wales and big cities like Liverpool, Newcastle and Sheffield. If, on the other hand, the Conservatives move back towards the centre, and the Labour Government's popularity goes on waning, the possibility of a hung Parliament looms once again.

And what if Britain did adopt a proportional system? The pressures under those circumstances would undoubtedly become increasingly strong for the Conservative Party to split. The Pro-Euro Conservative Party, founded by the former Euro-MPs John Stevens and Brendan Donnelly, never really stood a chance under a 'first past the post' system. Instead, its former members are proving a great asset to the Liberal Democrats.

There are other Conservatives, however, who are profoundly unhappy with the turn which the party Leadership has taken, but who neverthe-less see themselves very firmly in the Conservative rather than the Liberal tradition. Traditional Conservatism sets as much store by social networks as it does by political ideas. There are Conservatives who would agree with almost all the Liberal Democrat manifesto who would never bring themselves to leave the Tory Party.

Such people might, however, be very attracted to a new moderate Conservative Party. At the same time, it is possible to envisage circumstances under which the Labour left splits off to form its own party. Under the proposals of the 1999 Jenkins Commission on PR, some general elections would produce an outright majority for a single party, but most would not. It would be feasible in these balanced Parliaments to imagine the Liberal Democrats having a choice of potential partners in Government between moderate Conservatives and moderate Labour parties.

It is easy to go on speculating. Numerous scenarios are possible. The fate of the Liberal Democrats, as always in the past, at the mercy to some extent of the successes and failures of its opponents. But there are important differences from the previous occasions when breakthrough seemed possible.

The party's current position is the result of a slow and steady build-up during a period which has lasted over a decade. It is entirely different in character from the sudden surge that accompanied the birth of the SDP. It means that there are now elected Liberal Democrat representatives in almost every part of the country. They have had time to build up solid reputations locally. Many of them run local authorities and there are three Liberal Democrat Cabinet ministers in Scotland. One of the greatest handicaps which the party has had in the past has been the perception, fostered heavily by its opponents, that Liberal Democrats cannot win. There is now a substantial body of evidence to refute this claim. The party now has far more credibility than it has ever had.

When the Parliamentary Party grew to over fifty MPs, it achieved a critical mass which it did not have before. With more MPs, the Liberal Democrats are more visible in the House of Commons and better placed to command media attention. Meanwhile the party's members of the European Parliament are the largest national contingent in the ELDR group, which effectively holds the balance of power, and Liberal Democrat peers can often prove to be crucial swing voters in the House of Lords. The party has far more influence at every level of national politics than it had when breakthrough appeared possible in the past.

Then there is the state of the electorate. It is much more volatile than it has ever been before. As class loyalties become less and less relevant, neither the Conservatives nor the Labour Party can count on the solid bedrock support which they used to have. The concepts of left- and right-wing are becoming increasingly meaningless. At the same time, the general disillusionment with politics affects the old parties much more than the Liberal Democrats. It opens up a huge opportunity for a party like Charles Kennedy's to present a fresh and different face to the voters.

After 1962, both the Conservative and Labour, each with a new leader, recovered rapidly. After 1981 the Conservatives regained support because of the Falklands War. This time it is not obvious how either of these parties can transform their fortunes before a general election in 2005 or 2006.

The Liberal Democrats are beter placed now to exploit a favourable political situation than they were in the past. Campaigning techniques are more sophisticated and the party as a whole is considerably more professional than it used to be. It has also more coherance and a clear sense of direction. Ther is no sign of the drift which occurred between the two 1974 elections or of a major internal argument like the row over defence in 1986.

Because the advance this time has been slow and steady rather than precipitate and spectacular, it is not generating the level of excitement of 1962 or 1981. Nonetheless the party does have greater appeal to young people. Polling carried out in 2003 suggests that it is ahead of the Conservatives in every age group below forty-five. It helps to have a leader who appeals to people who do not have much time for conventional politicians.

There are still handicaps. The Liberal Democrats have nothing like the financial resources of either the Conservatives or Labour. Central

Office and Millbank Tower each spent seven times as much as Cowley Street in the 2001 general election. The party also lacks sufficient activist members. It has proved that with a core of enthusiasts it is capable of winning almost any kind of local government ward, from the richest rural area to the poorest inner-city district. As yet, there are not enough people in enough places who are willing to put in the work. Moreover, Liberal Democrats are not always as good as they should be at holding on to ground which they have won. At general elections and by-elections in the post-war period, they and their predecessor parties have won around a hundred different parliamentary seats, but they have gone on to lose almost half of them.

In February 2001, before the general election, MORI asked the standard polling question about how people intended to vote. The answer was 13% Liberal Democrat. They then asked a follow-up question. 'If you thought the Liberal Democrats could win in your constituency, how would you vote?' The change was astonishing: 36% said Liberal Democrat, 36% said Labour and 23% said Conservative. The more the party can establish its credibility as a potential winner, the more those votes will be won.

There is a long way to go. There will be twists and turns and setbacks on the way. But the opportunities are enormous. There is no guarantee at all anymore that the pattern of British politics which persisted through most of the twentieth century will last very long into the twenty-first.

Selected Bibliography

Paddy Ashdown: *Diaries* Vol 1 and Vol 2, Allen Lane, 2000 and 2001.

Peter Bartram: *David Steel: His life and times in politics*, Star 1981.

Duncan Brack and Tony Little eds: *Great Liberal Speeches*, Politico's 2001.

Ian Bradley: *Breaking the Mould*, Martin Robertson 1981.

David Butler: *The British General Election* series, Macmillan:

   with Anthony King 1964, 1966;

   with Michael Pinto-Duschinsky 1970;

   with Dennis Kavanagh February 1974, October 1974, 1979, 1983, 1987, 1992, 1997 and 2001.

John Callaghan: *Socialism in Britain*, Blackwell 1990.

Arthur Cyr: *Liberal Party Politics in Britain*, John Calder 1977.

George Dangerfield: *The Strange Death of Liberal England*, MacGibbon and Kee 1935.

Roy Douglas: *The History of the Liberal Party 1895–1970*, Sidgwick and Jackson 1971.

Roy Jenkins: *Asquith*, Collins 1964.

Roy Jenkins: *A Life at the Centre*, Macmillan 1991.

Roy Jenkins: *Partnership of Principle*, edited by Clive Lindley, Secker and Warburg 1985.

The Journal of Liberal Democrat History and the *Journal of Liberal History* (passim).

Charles Kennedy: *The Future of Politics*, Harper Collins 2000.

Ludovic Kennedy: *On My Way to the Club*, Collins 1989.

Anthony King and Ivor Crewe: *SDP: The birth, life and death of the Social Democratic Party*, Oxford 1995.

Don MacIver ed: *The Liberal Democrats*, Prentice Hall 1996.

Michael McManus: *Jo Grimond: Towards the sound of gunfire*, Birlinn 2001.

John Major: *Autobiography*, Harper Collins 1999.

Alistair Michie and Simon Hoggart: *The Pact*, Quartet 1978.

David Owen: *Time to Declare*, Michael Joseph 1991.

Rachael Pitchford and Tony Greaves: *Merger, the Inside Story*, Liberal Renewal 1989.

Chris Rennard: *Winning Local Elections*, ALC 1988.

Bill Rodgers: *Fourth Among Equals*, Politico's 2000.

Donald Sassoon: *100 Years of Socialism*, Fontana 1996.

David Steel: *Against Goliath*, Weidenfeld and Nicholson, 1989.

David Steel: *The Decade of Re-alignment: The leadership speeches of David Steel*, ed Stuart Mole, Hebden Royd 1986.

Jeremy Thorpe: *In My Own Time*, Politico's 1999.

Des Wilson: *Battle For Power: The inside story of the Alliance and the 1987 General Election*, Sphere 1987.

Index